T0300333

Quality of the Environment

Contemporary society is dependent on man's ability to work fundamental changes in the natural environment. In using resources to produce high and rising levels of income, however, effects are often
produced that are incidental to the main purpose. This study, first
published in 1965, explores some research approaches to the economic
analysis of some of the key environmental problems, including water
and air pollution, the introduction of chemical substances into the
environment and the development of urban and rural space. This title
will be of interest to students of environmental studies and economics.

Quality of the Environment

An Economic Approach to Some Problems in
Using Land, Water, and Air

Orris C. Herfindahl
Allen V. Kneese

First published in 1965
by Resources for the Future, Inc.

This edition first published in 2015 by Routledge
2 Park Square, Milton Park, Abingdon, Oxon, OX14 4RN
and by Routledge
711 Third Avenue, New York, NY 10017

Routledge is an imprint of the Taylor & Francis Group, an informa business

© 1965 Resources for the Future, Inc.

Publisher's Note
The publisher has gone to great lengths to ensure the quality of this reprint but points out that some imperfections in the original copies may be apparent.

Disclaimer
The publisher has made every effort to trace copyright holders and welcomes correspondence from those they have been unable to contact.

A Library of Congress record exists under LC control number: 65024756

ISBN 13: 978-1-138-93626-3 (hbk)
ISBN 13: 978-1-315-67693-7 (ebk)

QUALITY
OF THE
ENVIRONMENT:

An Economic Approach to
Some Problems in Using
Land, Water, and Air

by ORRIS C. HERFINDAHL
and ALLEN V. KNEESE

RESOURCES FOR THE FUTURE, INC.
1755 Massachusetts Avenue, N.W., Washington, D.C. 20036

Distributed by THE JOHNS HOPKINS PRESS
Baltimore and London

Resources for the Future is a nonprofit corporation for research and education in the development, conservation, and use of natural resources and the
improvement of the quality of the environment. It was established in 1952
with the co-operation of the Ford Foundation. Part of the work of Resources for the Future is carried out by its resident staff; part is supported
by grants to universities and other nonprofit organizations. Unless otherwise stated, interpretations and conclusions in RFF publications are those
of the authors; the organization takes responsibility for the selection of
significant subjects for study, the competence of the researchers, and their
freedom of inquiry.

Orris C. Herfindahl is a senior research associate with RFF; Allen V.
Kneese is director of RFF's program of studies in the quality of the environment.

RFF staff editors: Henry Jarrett, Vera W. Dodds, Nora E. Roots, Tadd
Fisher.

PREFACE

The perennial popular question about natural resource products is, "When are we going to 'run out'?" Stated in this way, the question is overly naive unless our horizon is very distant. But long before we are aware of an impending "running out" we may come to be acutely aware of something else that is happening to us, a gradually growing stream of stimuli that produce an increasing dissatisfaction and, unfortunately, a dissatisfaction with which the individual finds it very hard to cope. What we have in mind perhaps can be summed up by saying that it may well be our lot to suffer a deterioration in the "quality of the environment." This phrase suffers from the most serious analytical defects; yet it seems to evoke response and understanding in the minds of many who hear and use it.

Whatever the merits of the phrase, our concern is that certain problems of market failure, as they are called by the economist, will become radically more serious as time goes on. But how could this be so in a society that is so obviously progressing—as measured by the gross national product? Apart from the obvious observation that the GNP does not and can not possibly measure everything that is relevant to our feeling of well-being, many of our activities of production, movement, and consumption do, unfortunately, inflict unwanted penalties on others. Water pollution carried to the downstream user is the stock example, but it is only one of a much larger class. In many important cases, these unwanted effects are taken account of very inadequately or not at all by our politico-economic system.

Our fear is that such effects may grow in importance as population and incomes increase, to the point where we shall be all too conscious of a deterioration in the quality of the environment.

Whatever the degree of deterioration that is in prospect for us—and opinions differ widely on this, often reflecting radically differing tastes—it is our view that economic reasoning can make a substantial contribution to the handling of these problems. This is not a task for economics alone, for it is obvious that the collaboration of many other disciplines is required if the analysis of any one of these problems is to be useful.

We feel, however—and the reader should be warned that we are economists—that the discipline of economics is central to progress on these problems, for it is economics alone that can formulate these problems in the terms to which they must finally be reduced, namely the balancing of our varied desires in these matters against the costs of satisfying them in various degrees.

Accordingly, our purpose is twofold: We seek to show the non-economist why economic reasoning is not only helpful but indispensable in the analysis of these problems. We also seek to give the economist some understanding of the intriguing non-economic substance of these problems. We hope to interest him to the point where he will be moved to make an applied or perhaps even a theoretical contribution.

Clearly we have erected two stools. It is our hope that we have also erected a bridge.

·   ·   ·   ·   ·   ·

This study owes a major debt to Irving K. Fox. Our views on the problems examined reflect a long period of continuing discussion with him, a discussion that has often stimulated re-examination and reformulation. We are grateful, also, for helpful comments from Edward O. Banfield, Blair Bower, Robert K. Davis, John R. Goldsmith, J. Charles Headley, Edgar M. Hoover, and A. Allan Schmid. The study was a part of the work done in preparation for a new area of research at Resources for the Future, following some work already done in studies of water pollution and pesticides.

ORRIS C. HERFINDAHL AND ALLEN V. KNEESE

CONTENTS

CHAPTER I

INTRODUCTION: FIVE
ENVIRONMENTAL PROBLEMS

Contemporary society is dependent on man's ability to work fundamental changes in the natural environment. Indeed, this society could not exist without large-scale clearing of forested land and plowing of prairies, without substantial changes in natural drainage systems, and without the conversion of rural landscapes into the compact urban places essential for many industrial and commercial processes.

In using resources to produce high and rising levels of income, however, effects are often produced that are incidental to the main purpose. Some of these "side effects," as they might be called, go beyond the economic unit that produces them and may affect others in important ways—some favorably and some unfavorably. Such effects may be thought of as a part of the environment in which we work and produce.

It is obvious that the economy is full of these side effects. Most of them are inconsequential or are unavoidable, for to live in and participate in a society necessarily exposes us to the activities of others in ways that are beyond control—whether our own individual control or the control of society. Some of these effects are easily controllable, however, and the impact of others is so serious that our best effort to ameliorate them is warranted.

As yet, little has been done to bring economic analysis to bear on environmental problems; hence, in this study, which explores some research approaches, we have rather arbitrarily selected five study areas each very different from the other but all sharing the

1

common problems generated by external effects: that is, in every case the actions of certain economic units are seriously affecting the use of the environment by other businesses and individuals.[1] The numbers affected are large and the effects are sizable, whether taken as a whole or restricted to each economic unit. The problem areas are:

1. Water pollution;
2. Air pollution;
3. The purposeful introduction into the environment of chemical substances such as pesticides, insecticides, preservatives, coloring agents, etc.;
4. Some developments in urban activities, architecture, and the use of urban space;
5. Development of the rural countryside and "wild" areas.

The meager evidence bearing on trends in the five problem areas does not indicate that degradation of all aspects of the physical environment is continuous and inexorable. Serious deterioration in some aspects of environmental quality did take place between say, 1840 and 1940, but because in the process other values were created it is difficult to determine whether it was excessive. By most measures the quality of air and water deteriorated, sometimes severely. Wild areas were brought under development, and their beauty frequently was impaired or destroyed. Game populations diminished rapidly, and in many cases ugly and congested cities were created.

Since 1940, however, the quality of the environment has in some respects markedly improved. Rivers have been cleaned of their grossest floating materials; cities have substantially reduced the particulate matter in their atmosphere; some of the worst slums have been eliminated; public health, at least so far as infectious diseases are concerned, has been greatly improved; much land has been returned to a wild state, and many important varieties of wildlife have been encouraged to increase spectacularly.

[1] See the discussion of externalities and the significance of external effects, pp. 5–9.

As far as it goes, the record of the past twenty years has been good. What then are our problems today? First, we are still looking for systematic ways by which external effects of many activities can be evaluated and enlightened decisions made. Second, the processes affecting the quality of the physical environment have become increasingly subtle: Compare, for instance, some that have been controlled to a major extent—human excrement floating in streams and estuaries, or coal dust sullying the air—with others that confront us today—the invisible persistent organic chemicals that are in solution in rivers, or the tasteless, odorless, colorless carbon monoxide and dioxide that damage the atmosphere. Third, the demand for a "good" physical environment can be expected to grow much faster than population and even than per capita income. This is already apparent in one area where there is fairly direct evidence, that of outdoor recreation. Indeed, the present concern with environmental quality may stem as much or more from increased demands as from deterioration in supply. Several types of increased demand have, for example, been associated with the large growth in automobile ownership. Fourth, complexity, growing demands, and the increasing geographical scope of the problems, as well as the diffuseness of costs imposed, cast doubt upon the adequacy of present institutional arrangements to deal with these problems.

To a large extent, individuals or households, rather than businesses, receive the direct effects of these environmental hazards. In the areas of water and air pollution, for example, a good many pollutants directly affect the health of individuals who have had no transaction with the "producer" of the pollutant. Here the flow of stimuli to the affected parties involves the transmission of physical particles.

In other problem areas, however, it is not health as such, but the preferences of individuals which may be affected either directly or by altering the prices of goods and services. Such cases—in which health is not directly affected—may sometimes involve the transmission of physical bodies and sometimes only the flow of visual, aural, or olfactory impressions.

Finally, there are external effects of which the individual may be unaware but which may be of considerable importance to his well-being. One common example is the complex set of stimuli flowing to the individual from his urban environment. Even when the existence of these stimuli is consciously recognized, their effects on the psyche are often very imperfectly perceived by the persons affected.

Admittedly, the two general categories of external effects that have been distinguished here—the "direct" effects on health and those effects that involve preferences—are not completely independent. Individual preferences with respect to health in combination with factors affecting it may differ. And for many people, health itself can be affected by the psychic satisfactions and dissatisfactions they experience. In spite of these considerations, the distinction appears to be an important and useful one, because the means for analyzing and dealing with the two categories are likely to be quite different.

TOOLS FOR ANALYZING
SOME ENVIRONMENTAL PROBLEMS

While diverse in many respects, the problem areas selected for discussion in this study do have much in common—in origin, diagnosis, and treatment. To see why this is so, we must re-examine some fundamentals of economics to show how a market system operates under two different sets of basic conditions. Let us look at the following two cases:

1. A hypothetical system in which the activities of the different economic units are independent of each other in a "real" sense. That is, a change in the output or activity of a firm (or person) does not *entail* a change in the output of any other firm or in the satisfaction experienced by an individual.

2. A system in which activities of some economic units are partially but not completely independent.

Case 1. Independent Economic Activities. Under certain conditions a market economy will produce precisely those goods and services wanted by consumers, produce these in just the quantities wanted, and produce these quantities in the cheapest possible way. One of the important conditions for this result is that economic activities be independent in a "real" sense. In other words, it is a condition where quantities of *all* parts of an individual's consumption are under his control and *all* the inputs of each business, such as labor, services of machines, etc., are under its control. If we further imagine an economy not disturbed by the introduction of new methods of production or changes in consumer tastes, an economy in which both consumers and producers know what they are doing and in which no industry is dominated by a few firms, we can envision a succession of adjustments which would yield these happy results. Adam Smith, who was perhaps the first to perceive clearly the possibility of an economic system functioning in this way, described the process as the market's "invisible hand." The importance of this perception remains undiminished even today, for it serves to isolate for us and permit us to understand the basic function of a market economy—the organization of production so as to produce what each consumer wants produced within the limit of his income.

Things actually don't work out quite that way, a fact which will surprise no one who is exposed to the day-by-day operations of the economy. In order to construct on paper an abstract model of the economy which will clearly exhibit these properties, it is necessary to imagine a world which is different from the real world. But the automatic functioning of the invisible hand of the market, which can be seen so clearly in this simplified model, becomes obscured when we look at the real world and ask how well the economy succeeds in producing what is wanted. While observers differ on the degree to which the economy falls short in performing this function, all are agreed that it does fall short.

Case 2. Externalities. Some reasons for this less-than-perfect operation of the economy are clear. Technological change and changes in consumer tastes are disturbing factors that can bring problems of adjustment. Consumer or producer ignorance may prevent people from doing as well as they might with the resources at their command. But of equal importance is the fact that what a consumer consumes or what a business firm uses is not entirely within its control. That is, there are flows of some goods or services that come to the consumer or business whether he wants them or not and without his paying for them. This situation may be described by saying that a change in the output of one economic unit (a firm or consumer) necessarily affects the inputs (and hence the output) of some other economic unit. That is, the activities of one economic unit may generate "real" effects that are external to it. These effects are often called external effects, or "externalities." It is exactly this which characterizes each of the problem areas discussed in these pages. For example, an increase in the output of a cannery may increase stream pollution, which in turn will require downstream firms or communities to spend more money to clean up the water they use. They have experienced an unwanted increase of certain inputs—pollutants in this case.

Thus it is evident that the activities of any kind of economic unit, whether a family, a business firm, or a governmental unit, may generate direct, or external, effects on other economic units. The variety of possible cases is very great, and the range of problems and possible solutions is correspondingly great. The number of other economic units affected may vary from one to all in the economy. The damages (or benefits) inflicted may not vary with the output of the initiating unit (damages may be constant) or they may increase in various ways as output of the initiator changes. At one extreme stands a "pure" case, one in which the effects of an economic unit's activity are wholly external to that unit and are available to anyone and everyone. Such effects have come to be called "public goods." Stock examples are certain governmental services such as the provision of defense or the legal system. Such services have the peculiar property that my consumption of them does not diminish yours. Hence it is impractical to get very many people to pay "voluntarily" for their consumption of these services. We therefore voluntarily decide through the political system to require payment in the form of taxes for the support of such services. Some of the cases discussed in this study have something of a public good aspect about them. This complicates their treatment and makes certain remedies impractical.

The Significance of External Effects. If external effects are present, a misallocation of resources is likely to be the result whether the external effect is beneficial or detrimental to its recipient. The reason for this is that the signals which tell a firm how much it should produce—price and cost—may not work properly in the presence of external effects. With no external effects present, we may think of a firm comparing the price it will get from making and selling another unit of its produce with the associated cost. So long as price is greater than this cost, it will pay to expand output. When the two are equal, it will not pay to expand output any further, for that would diminish profit. This output happens also to be the right output from the point of view of the consumers viewed as a group, for the value of the article to them as measured by price is just equal to the costs of making it. These costs are equal to the value of other articles that could have been produced and hence measure what consumers had to give up in order to produce the article in question. If labor services are used to produce shoes, they can't be used to produce furniture.

If external effects are present, this nice balance may be upset. Suppose that a business pollutes a stream and that this increases the costs of treating water supplies downstream. If the business is not induced to take account of this effect, it will neglect these costs in deciding how much to produce. From the point of view of the consumers (again viewed as a group) the firm is producing too much, for the costs associated with the production of another unit of the business' product are now greater than its price. If all costs are taken into account, including the higher water treatment costs, consumers will be giving up other products that could have been produced (the value of which is measured by all costs) in return for a unit of product that is less valuable. This is a misallocation of production. Note that if the external effect had been beneficial the result would also have been a misallocation, but output of the product in question would have been too small rather than too large.

External effects may be generated and received by any pair of economic units. Smith's record player may disturb Jones's rest. Or their cars may slow each other and other drivers on the way to work. We may swim in or picnic alongside water that has been polluted by businesses, individuals, or even governmental units. In the case of the problems discussed here, individuals are important as recipients of the external effects involved.

Misallocation of production—this is the problem that may result when external effects are present. It does not follow, however, that detrimental external effects should be eliminated, for this might entail the elimination of other associated effects or products that are of greater value to consumers. In dealing with the allocation problem arising from external effects, the goal is to find some means whereby decisions on how much to produce take proper account of all the costs and benefits flowing from the economic activity in question. Within a static framework, there are three ways to get this result. One is for the unit(s) that generates the effect to come to agreement with the recipient(s) of the effect on the proper level of the effect—perhaps with a payment from one to the other. Where the effect is measurable and the number of units involved is small, this solution may be feasible.

A second method is to "internalize" the problem so that a single economic unit will take into account all of the costs and benefits associated with the effect. One way is to enlarge the size of the economic unit. For example, the same regional agency might be responsible for both sewage treatment and water supply. Another way to induce consideration of all costs and benefits is to change the limitations under which the initiator of the effect is operating. This could be done by imposing a tax or charge on the effect that is emitted (or a subsidy if the effect is beneficial), in which case the firm may decide to reduce the effect either by cutting the output of its main product or by spending some money to reduce the external effect, for example, by treating waste solutions in the plant. Still another way is to regulate the emission directly. For example, it might be required that an undesirable emission be kept below a certain specified level.

"Internalizing" the problem has the advantage of letting the economic units involved decide on the best adjustment to be made in the light of all costs and benefits. It may be possible and desirable to eliminate or reduce the effect, but there will be some cases in which the best thing to be done is simply to bear it.

A third method is to control production directly, perhaps by governmental operation of the activity that produces the external effect.

In the search for ways to improve the misallocation resulting from external effects, care must always be exercised to take into account any additional costs or penalties associated with the remedy. It is quite possible, for example, to set standards designed to reduce external effects so strict that there will be a loss to national product rather than a gain. Nor should it be assumed that other types of governmental regulations are costless, for they sometimes require large regulatory staffs and may involve other types of costs, some of which are not obvious and may be hard to measure.

There is one other way of dealing with externalities which may be usable in some cases but which goes beyond the static framework in which externalities are usually considered. It may be possible to conceive of new processes or new ways of organizing production so as to reduce or eliminate undesired external effects or to enhance desirable effects. The conception of new processes should be distinguished from different methods of production which are already known but whose use can be induced by, say, the imposition of a tax on the external effect. The distinction between the use of different methods already known and genuinely new methods is hazy both in theory and practice, but it is important to realize that substantial changes in production methods are sometimes possible if a way can be found to focus attention on the problem.

CHAPTER II

WATER POLLUTION

Although more may be known about water pollution than about any of the other environmental problems we shall discuss, generalization about it is hazardous because causes and effects vary greatly from region to region and because a complex variety of substances and biochemical reactions is involved. Let us look briefly at some of the major water pollutants and some of the concepts concerning them which the sanitary engineers and their colleagues in related sciences have developed.[1]

DEGRADABLE POLLUTANTS

Water pollutants may be classified as *degradable* or *non-degradable,* according to their behavior when they are discharged into a stream. The most widespread and best known degradable pollutant is domestic sewage, but in the aggregate industry produces greater amounts of organic waste, almost all of which is generated by the food, pulp and paper, and chemicals industries. Some industrial plants are fantastic producers of organic pollution: a single pulp mill, for example, can produce wastes equivalent to the sewage flow of a large city.

When an effluent bearing a substantial load of organic wastes is expelled into an otherwise clean stream, a process known as "aerobic degradation" begins immediately. Stream biota, primarily bacteria, feed on the wastes and break them down into their inorganic components (nitrogen, phosphorous, and carbon) which

---

[1] Klein in reference 2 presents an excellent detailed discussion of many of these matters. See Selected References at end of this chapter, p. 23.

are basic plant nutrients. In the breaking down of organic material, a process that is somewhat deceptively known as stream self-purification, some of the oxygen which is dissolved in any clean water is consumed. But this depletion tends to be offset by reoxygenation which occurs through the air-water interface and as a consequence of photosynthesis by the plants in the water. If the waste load is not too heavy, dissolved oxygen in the stream first will drop to a limited extent (say, to 4 or 5 parts per million from a saturation level of perhaps 8–10 ppm, depending upon temperature) and then rise again. This process can be described by a characteristically shaped curve or function known as the "oxygen sag."

If the organic waste in a stream becomes great enough, however, the process of degradation may exhaust the dissolved oxygen. In such cases degradation is still carried forward, but it takes place anaerobically, that is, through the action of bacteria which do not use free oxygen but organically or inorganically bound oxygen, common sources of which are nitrates and sulphates. Gaseous by-products result, among them methane and hydrogen sulfide.

Water in which wastes are being degraded anaerobically emits foul odors, looks black and bubbly, and aesthetically is altogether offensive. Indeed, the unbelievably foul odors from the Thames in mid-nineteenth century London caused the halls of Parliament to be hung with sheets soaked in quicklime and even induced recess upon occasion when the reek became too suffocating. So extreme a condition is rarely encountered nowadays, but levels of dissolved oxygen low enough to kill fish and cause other ecological changes are still frequent.

High temperatures accelerate degradation. Thus a waste-load which would not induce low levels of dissolved oxygen at one temperature may do so if the temperature of the water rises. In such circumstances heat may be considered a pollutant. Huge amounts of heat are put into streams by the cooling water effluents of industry. Steam electric power plants, whose output is increasing rapidly, pose a special problem, for even now they use more water than all industries and municipalities combined.

The ordinary sewage treatment plant uses the same processes which occur naturally in a stream, but by careful control they are greatly speeded up. Under most circumstances sewage treatment plants are capable of reducing the BOD (biochemical oxygen demand) in waste effluent by perhaps 90 per cent. As with degradation occurring in a water course, plant nutrients are the end product of the process.

It has been pointed out that the excessive organic waste-loads associated with anaerobic degradation make a stream unfit for any use except as a sewer. But where low levels of free oxygen (not zero) are present in a stream, much can be done to make the water usable for a variety of purposes, though the problems are complex. Let us glance briefly at some of these problems. Although aesthetic quality largely governs the utility of water-based recreation, low levels of dissolved oxygen need not prevent people from enjoying some activities, such as boating and swimming, even though the ecological effect may be profound. On the other hand, extensive stretches of streams which persistently carry less than 4 or 5 ppm of oxygen will not support the higher forms of fish life. Even where they are not lethal, reduced levels of oxygen increase the sensitivity of fish to toxins. Water in which the organic waste has not been completely stabilized is more costly to treat for public or industrial supplies. This is because more chlorine is required to achieve the "free-chlorine residual" necessary to kill bacteria. Finally, the plant nutrients produced by bacterial degradation of organic wastes may cause algae blooms. Up to a certain level algae growth in a stream is not harmful and may even increase fish food, but larger amounts can be toxic, produce odors, reduce the river's aesthetic appeal, and increase treatment problems. Difficulties with algae are likely to become severe only when waste-loads have become large enough to require high levels of treatment. Then residual plant nutrient products become abundant relative to streamflow and induce excessive plant growth.

Problems of this kind are particularly important in comparatively quiet waters such as lakes and tidal estuaries. In recent years certain Swiss and American lakes have changed their character radically because of the buildup of plant nutrients. The possibility of excessive algae growth is one of the unresolved problems in planning for pollution abatement in the Potomac and other estuaries, for effective treatment processes today carry a high price tag. Two extremely important challenges to research are to find improved means of removing plant nutrients from sewage effluent and of predicting with more accuracy the conditions under which algae grow and the effects they have on water.

The magnitude of our present and future water pollution problem is imperfectly indicated by some historical records of the BOD in terms of population equivalents (i.e., the oxygen-demanding effects of the untreated organic wastes of one person) and by some BOD load projections into the future. The figures on BOD from industry are extremely undependable, and the projections typically neglect all means of reduction (like industrial process and product changes) except treatment. With these qualifications in mind, one can learn from Table 1 something of the range of growth of BOD as envisioned by the U.S. Public Health Service. What happens to BOD in the years to come obviously depends largely on the extent to which wastes are treated before they enter streams. On one set of assumptions,[2] involving considerable growth in treatment facilities, BOD would actually decline at about 2 per cent per year between 1960 and 1980 in contrast to increases in the past half-century of considerably more than 2 per cent per year. On the other hand, continuation of present rates of construction of treatment facilities[3] results in an estimated growth of BOD of about 3½ per cent per year.

Bacteria might also be included among what we have called the degradable pollutants since the enteric infectious type die off rather quickly in a stream, and treatment with chlorine is highly effective against them. Thus the traditional scourges of polluted water—typhoid, paratyphoid, dysentery, gastroenteritis —have become almost unknown in municipal areas in this country. Viruses, on the other hand, some of which are more viable than

[2] See footnotes 2 and 5 of Table 1.
[3] See footnotes 4 and 6 of Table 1.

QUALITY OF THE ENVIRONMENT

bacteria outside the body environment, are apparently less responsive to treatment and have become a source of concern to public health officials. Some believe that viruses in water supplies are associated with the spread of certain diseases at less than epidemic levels rather than being epidemiological problems as some bacteria once were.

TABLE 1. POPULATION EQUIVALENT BIOCHEMICAL OXYGEN DEMAND DISCHARGED BY MUNICIPALITIES AND INDUSTRIES

(in millions)

Year	Municipal population equivalent discharged	Industrial population equivalent discharged
1900	24.0	15
1920	40.0	49
1935	51.0	
1940		75
1950	60.0	100
1959		150
1960	75.0	
1970	[1]76.0	[2]50
	[3]84.0	[4]210
1980	[5]74.0	[2]80
	[6]150.0	[4]310

[1] Assumes that progress towards secondary treatment for all municipal wastes by 1980 will be made; a per capita population equivalent (P.E.) of 1.6; and 80% removal of P.E. by secondary treatment.

[2] Assumes that 80% removal of population equivalent by treatment will be obtained.

[3] Same as note 1 above, except assumes present rate of sewage treatment.

[4] Assumes that the current estimated percentage rate of growth of industrial wastes treatment construction will continue.

[5] Assumes that all sewered population will be served by secondary sewage treatment by 1980; a per capita population equivalent (P.E.) of 1.75; and 80% removal of P.E. by secondary treatment.

[6] Same as note 5 above, except assumes that present rate of sewage treatment construction will continue.

Source: U.S. Public Health Service; and unpublished data from the Service's Basin Data Branch, Division of Water Supply and Pollution Control, reported in Stein (reference 5), pp. 397–98.

NON-DEGRADABLE POLLUTANTS

BOD serves as an indicator of the extent of the pollution problem where one aspect is concerned—the degradable pollutants. But it will be recalled that some pollutants are non-degradable. These are not attacked by stream biota and undergo no great change once they get into a stream. In other words, the stream does not "purify itself" of them. This category includes inorganic substances—such materials as inorganic colloidal matter, ordinary salt, and the salts of numerous heavy metals. When these substances are present in fairly large quantities they result in toxicity, unpleasant taste, hardness, and, especially when chlorides are present, in corrosion. It is these pollutants that are partially or wholly responsible for corrosion, scaling, and pitting of industrial equipment such as pipes, water heaters, boilers, and rollers in steel rolling mills. They necessitate the use of water softeners, distilled water, and extra soap, and add considerably to the expense of treating industrial water supplies. To take care of them, our society relies heavily on the dilution capacity of receiving waters.

PERSISTENT POLLUTANTS

There is a third group of pollutants, of relatively recent origin, which does not fit comfortably into either the degradable or nondegradable categories. These "persistent" or "exotic" pollutants are best exemplified by the synthetic organic chemicals produced in profusion by modern chemical industry. They enter water courses as effluent of industry and also as waste residuals from many household and agricultural uses. These substances are termed "persistent" because stream biota cannot effectively attack their complex molecular chains. Some degradation does take place, but usually so slowly that the persistents travel long stream distances in virtually unchanged form. Detergents (e.g., ABS), pesticides (e.g., DDT), and phenols (resulting from the distillation of petroleum and coal products) are among the most common of these pollutants. Fortunately, the recent development and successful manufacture of "soft" or degradable detergents has opened the way toward reduction or elimination of the problems associated with them, especially that of foaming.[4]

Some of the persistent organics, like phenols and hard detergents, present primarily aesthetic problems. The phenols, for example, can cause an unpleasant taste in waters. Others are under suspicion as possible public health problems and are associated with periodic fish kills in streams. Some of the new insecticides are unbelievably toxic. The material Endrin, which commonly has been used as an insecticide and rodenticide, is toxic to fish in minute concentrations. It has been calculated, for example, that 0.005 of a pound of Endrin in three acres of water one foot deep is acutely toxic to fish.[5]

Concentrations of the persistent organic substances have seldom if ever risen to levels in public water supplies high enough to present an *acute* danger to public health. The public health problem centers around the possible *chronic* effects of prolonged exposure to very low concentrations. Similarly, even in concentrations too low to be acutely poisonous to fish, these pollutants may have profound effects on stream ecology.

No solid evidence implicates present concentrations of organic chemicals in water supplies as a cause of health problems, but some experts are suspicious of them. Several public health officials, for example, feel they may be linked to cancer, and Nobel prize-winning geneticist H. J. Muller questions whether they may not be involved in undesirable genetic mutations.[6] It has been demonstrated that concentrated raw and finished water supplies have carcinogenic effects when injected into test animals, but the truth is that we don't know enough about the effects of these chemicals. This knowledge is very difficult and very expensive to come by.

[4] For further information see statement of Dr. R. B. Wearm in reference 6 at p. 1055.
[5] From statement by Dr. Clarence Cottam in reference 4, at p. 227. Further discussion of the effects on wildlife of purposeful introduction of toxins into the environment is presented in Chapter IV.
[6] In a letter to Allen V. Kneese.

There are presently some 500,000 organic chemicals known, most of them synthetically produced. Hundreds of organic chemicals are present in *treated* water supplies at low concentrations. Identification is costly, and typically, therefore, it is not known what chemicals in what concentrations are present. Chronic toxicity tests are very expensive—reported figures run from $50,000 to $250,000 per compound. Perhaps even more germane is the shortage of specialists in toxicology. Increase in skilled research and expanded work in this area is urgently needed. The recently revised PHS drinking water standards contain an aggregate standard for all *synthetic* dissolved organic substances that can be extracted from the water by a carbon filter. However, this standard, which is 200 ppb (higher than concentrations currently found in public supplies), has little meaning with respect to chronic toxicity since it is based upon the threshold where tastes and odors become apparent. Toxic effects may occur at lower levels.

The long-lived radio-nuclides might also be included in the category of persistent pollutants. They are subject to degradation but at very low rates. Atomic power plants may be an increasingly important source of such pollutants. Generation of power by nuclear fission produces fission products which are contained in the fuel rods of reactors. In the course of time they are separated by chemical processes to recover plutonium or to prevent waste products from "poisoning" the reactor and reducing its efficiency. Such atomic waste can impose huge external costs unless disposed of safely. A large volume of low-level waste resulting from the day-to-day operation of reactors can for the time being be diluted and discharged into streams, but the "hot" waste, containing long-lived substances such as radioactive strontium, cesium, and carbon, is in a different category from any other pollutant. It has been calculated, for example, that the effluent created in reworking the elements in the reactor at Hanford, Washington, is so "hot" that if one gallon per day were put into the vast flow of the Columbia River it would raise the radioactivity of the water above permissible levels. There are now over 50 million gallons of such effluent in storage at Hanford.[7]

So far, the only practical disposal method for high-level wastes is permanent storage: there is not enough dilution capacity on earth for any large amount of them, and effective treatment has yet to be found. Much research is being devoted to this special class of pollutants. In spite of this, the costs of disposal and the requirements for local disposal opportunities seem to be rather casually dismissed in projections of atomic development.

WATER QUALITY AND HEALTH

The relationship between water quality and health is even more subtle than the above discussion may suggest, for the presence of some substances in water may have a beneficial effect on health. According to the recently revised standard work on water quality criteria, "Several investigations have found a negative correlation between hardness in the drinking water of an area and death rates from degenerative cardiovascular disease, i.e., softer water was associated with higher death rates. These variations are unexplained on dietary, racial, or social bases. They have been observed in Japan, England, South Africa, the Canary Islands, Australia, and the U.S. Although the correlation appears to exist, its causative factors remained unexplained as of 1961."[8]

The investigative problem is further complicated by the fact that chemical substances enter the body in a variety of ways—water, air, food—in exceedingly complex combinations. To understand the interrelated effects of such combinations imaginative research is needed and this, as has been indicated, is limited more by the shortage of qualified personnel than by an absence of supporting funds.

----

[7] The cost of storage is considerable. If one adds "burial grounds" in Idaho and Georgia, the capital outlay comes to $200 million and yearly maintenance costs to $6 million. The life of the tanks is estimated at several decades. Ritchie Calder, *Living With the Atom* (Chicago: University of Chicago Press, 1962), pp. 203–5.

[8] Statement taken from reference 8.

AREAS WHERE RESEARCH IS NEEDED

On the basis of the foregoing discussion of water pollution, in which we have tried to identify major problem areas, several areas of needed research can be suggested.

1. *Gauging the Costs of Water Quality Deterioration.* As already noted, we are rapidly reaching a stage where in many streams at least the grossest and most obvious forms of pollution (floating materials—gross suspended matter) will have been dealt with. As a result, the situation presents some subtle questions. What quality of water is appropriate once the most blatantly offensive material is removed? Waste disposal is a highly valuable use of water courses. To what extent should we reduce this use now and in the future? How can we achieve a proper balance between the use of water courses for waste disposal and other valuable and usually conflicting uses such as municipal and industrial water supply and recreation?

These questions are becoming more and more complex, for we are entering into a whole new realm of effects and costs resulting from new types of wastes and increasingly heavy use of water courses. These effects and costs may be large in total magnitude, may affect large areas, and perhaps be reflected only slightly in the appearance of the water. They include treatment costs imposed on successive users, damages to facilities of various kinds, costs of going to alternative water supplies, and reduction of the value of water for recreational purposes. While evaluation is frequently difficult, methodology has developed sufficiently to hold good promise of providing useful values. This may be true even of recreation.

The task of measuring and forecasting the costs associated with water quality degradation has hardly begun. Virtually no dependable information of this kind is available to existing water quality control and planning efforts. And what is more, the value of certain aspects of health and aesthetics may never be reduced to satisfactory quantitative measurement. In these instances we may have to rely on standards which must be set without information on the value achieved by them. But often it will be possible to measure the values we *forego* because of the introduction of a standard. The least we can do in setting standards is to take account of the cost of achieving them. Unfortunately, standards now are usually set without reference to the values that must be foregone.

2. *Problems in Devising a System of Quality Control.* Once quality control moves beyond the point of removing floating and suspended materials from effluents, we have the opportunity to design systems of quality control which may be more efficient for the community, though they are more complex than simply treating wastes in industrial plants or in municipal sewage plants. For example, the fact that the level of streamflow may greatly affect water quality offers the opportunity to store seasonally high streamflows in reservoirs and release the water to augment lower flows, thereby improving quality, or to temporarily store wastes and release them when flows are high. Measures can be taken to enhance the self-purification capacity of receiving waters such as building shallow oxidation lakes in the streams themselves and/ or mechanically reaerating streams. Furthermore, a great variety of measures exist which involve industrial waste reclamation and process changes and offer ways of reducing industrial waste loads. In some circumstances the pattern of location of economic activities can be an important determinant of the cost of waste disposal and water supply facilities. The complicated interrelationships involved in these possibilities emphasize the necessity of taking a systematic regional view. Regulation of streamflow, for example, may alter water quality at remote locations downstream. If a quality control program is to have meaning, such effects must be foreseen and their benefits and penalties evaluated wherever these occur in the region. The problem is becoming one of regional water quality management rather than one of orthodox pollution control with its single-minded emphasis on treatment.

How can we design the best regional system for managing water quality? What kind of empirical information do we need?

How helpful can formal optimization approaches be? These questions increase in significance as abatement and damage costs rise.

Experience in the Ruhr area of Germany suggests that a thoroughgoing management system in highly developed basins will involve a variety of control measures. The Ruhr system, which has institutional arrangements permitting regional design and operation of the system, combines such large-scale measures as flow augmenation, treatment of entire streams, mechanical reaeration, and large collective treatment with conventional treatment plants at individual outfalls. Many of these possibilities are not systematically considered in planning for water quality control in the United States. Accordingly, little information exists on engineering economic feasibility. Case studies and demonstrations in some heavily developed smaller watersheds would be extremely valuable.

3. *Institutional Arrangements for Quality Management.* A third major problem is to devise appropriate institutional forms and tools of administration for management of water quality. In the past in this country we have relied heavily upon the civic responsibility of our citizens and on adversary proceedings to limit the quality degradation of streams.

The limitations of these devices have led us to go beyond them to direct administrative regulation of waste discharges from cities and industries, usually on the basis of general and quite arbitrary standards. In some basins, interstate compact authorities with advisory and limited enforcement powers have worked to establish at least minimum levels of treatment. In more recent years the federal government has provided financial assistance to local communities for the construction of waste treatment facilities. Also the federal government now provides low-flow augmentation from federal multipurpose reservoirs free of charge to local or state governments provided certain standards of treatment are met.

Are these the best institutional arrangements for obtaining optimal management of water quality? Or should we give serious thought to revising the governmental structures and management tools now used to control water quality? There is reason to believe, for example, that charges which vary with the kind and quantity of effluent may in some instances be superior to effluent standards for "internalizing" external costs because charges tend to give incentive to reduce waste where the costs of doing so are lowest. Research and demonstration projects focusing upon alternative means of regulation are urgently needed in this country. In heavily developed areas, institutions might be in order along the lines of the regional authorities in the Ruhr which have far-reaching power to design, construct, and operate regional systems. The new Delaware River Basin Commission may present an opportunity to move in this direction, as may also the new River Authorities in Great Britain.

Some Selected References on Water Pollution

1. Fair, Gordon Maskew and Geyer, John Charles. *Water Supply and Waste Disposal*. New York: John Wiley and Sons, 1956.
2. Klein, Louis. *River Pollution II: Causes and Effects*. London: Butterworths, 1962.
3. Kneese, Allen V. *The Economics of Regional Water Quality Management*. Baltimore: The Johns Hopkins Press for Resources for the Future, Inc., 1964.
4. *Proceedings—The National Conference on Water Pollution*. U.S. Department of Health, Education, and Welfare, Public Health Service. Washington: U.S. Government Printing Office, 1961.
5. Stein, Murray. "Problems and Programs in Water Pollution," *Natural Resources Journal*, December 1962.
6. *Water Pollution Control and Abatement*. (Part 1A, National Survey.) Hearings before a Subcommittee of the Committee on Government Operations, House of Representatives, 88th Congress, 1st Session. Washington: U.S. Government Printing Office, 1964.
7. *Water Pollution Control and Abatement*. (Part 1B, National Survey.)
8. *Water Quality Criteria*. California Water Quality Control Board, Sacramento, Calif., 1964.

CHAPTER III

AIR POLLUTION

In several recorded instances air pollution has reached deadly levels. There is the case of the Meuse Valley in Belgium, where in 1930, a hundred persons were made ill and sixty-three died. A similar situation occurred in this country in 1948, when fog and a low-level temperature inversion covered the horseshoe-shaped valley of the Monongahela River in Pennsylvania. Here, in the valley area around the town of Donora, nearly half the population became ill and twenty people died. In London during two weeks of December 1952, an estimated 4,000 deaths were recorded beyond those normal for the period. London was hit again in December of 1962, when more than 300 people died from the effects of air pollution—at about the same time that a national air pollution conference was being held in the United States.[1]

But occasional instances of deadly gases and particles engulfing a city do not begin to define the magnitude of the problem. The greatest health problems and the greatest property damage appear to arise from persistent exposure. One Public Health Service survey has indicated that in varying degrees air pollution affects at least 6,000 American communities. The effects may be highly localized, as where a single factory chimney belches smoke and gases. Or, as with the smog of Los Angeles, they may involve entire metropolitan areas. The character of air pollution has undergone such radical change in recent years that it is not possible to formulate a simple meaningful index of past change in magnitude.

---

[1] Fair in reference 4, and statement by Vernon G. MacKenzie (Chief, Division of Air Pollution, U.S. Public Health Service) in reference 2. See Selected References at end of this chapter, p. 34.

PRIMARY POLLUTANTS

Air polluting substances often are divided into two categories. The first of these consists of stable primary pollutants that are not changed in the air and consequently are comparatively easily traced to their source. These arise from industrial, commercial, domestic, transport, and agricultural activities, and are in the form of dust, smoke, fumes, and droplets (aerosols). They obscure sunlight and decrease visibility, they dirty buildings and other articles, corrode metals, and affect life processes. In the United States, coal burning used to be responsible for large amounts of primary pollutants, and it still is the major source of air pollution in many parts of Europe.

An extreme example of this type of pollution occurs in the Ruhr Basin of West Germany, which is intensively industrialized and heavily populated. There is a large and especially concentrated industrial complex stretching along the Rhine from Duisburg to Dinslagen. Despite efforts of the land planning authority for the Ruhr area to separate industrial from residential activities, this heavily industrialized area still contains a considerable residential population.

In addition to the interesting fact that waiters in Duisburg restaurants must change their collars three times a day, a study by Klaus-Peter Faerber (chief of the health agency in Oberhausen) and Alex Hoffman (section chief in the Hygienic Institute of Gelsenkirchen)[2] reports that over 15 per cent of the children in the Ruhr area show symptoms of rickets as against half this percentage in a control city situated in the Rhine Valley. The study also states that teen-age children in the Ruhr weigh less and are shorter than children in the control city. These physiological changes are not the only apparent results of air pollution;[3] there is also a large amount of property damage. It should be noted, of course, that substantial reduction of pollution discharge in this mammoth industrial area might be extremely expensive.

[2] Reported in *Der Spiegel* (Hamburg), August 9, 1961, p. 23.
[3] No doubt other factors are involved besides air pollution.

In recent years primary particulate forms of pollution in the United States have greatly declined. Between 1928 and 1962, for example, dust fall in Chicago decreased from an average of 395 tons per square mile per month to 43 tons;[4] and there is said to have been a comparable decline in dust fall throughout the country. The national monitoring network of the Public Health Service shows that suspended particulate matter in the atmosphere decreased between 1957 and 1961. A study by the U.S. Weather Bureau indicates that visibility is improving in many of the nation's urban areas.

The reduction in particulate matter and primary pollutants results basically from two causes. One is a greater use of liquid and gaseous fuels; the other is large-scale introduction of abatement devices by industry, especially the steel industry. However, the shift to the newer fuels is by no means an unmixed blessing, for the pollutants arising from them are in some respects more difficult to deal with than were the old types of pollutants. The residuals from the combustion of the newer fuels are particularly important contributors to the other major class of air pollutants known as secondary pollutants.

SECONDARY POLLUTANTS

Generally speaking, secondary pollutants are more intractable, have less predictable effect, and possibly are more dangerous to health than primary pollutants. They do not arise directly from any industrial, municipal, or household source, but are produced by photochemical or physicochemical interactions between primary pollutants within the atmosphere. The most objectionable pollutants of this type appear to arise from the oxidation (often produced by ozone which is generated by photochemical reaction between organic substances and oxides of nitrogen) of hydrocarbons which are present in incompletely burned fuel fumes. Some combinations of gaseous and particulate pollution have been shown experimentally to be capable of producing greater effects than the sum of the two types of pollutants separately. Much of

---

[4] Statement of Erwin E. Schulze in reference 2.

this work has been done with sulfur dioxide, which is often emitted with soots. These combinations appear to be sensitive to the relative humidity of the atmosphere.

An extreme example of secondary pollution is Los Angeles smog, which is largely the result of unburned fuels irradiated in stagnant air by sunlight. There are over 3 million automobiles in Los Angeles County which consume well over 6 million gallons of gasoline a day. The latest figures of the Los Angeles Air Pollution Control District (January 1963) indicate that the 3 million cars emit some 8,050 tons of carbon monoxide and almost 1,650 tons of hydrocarbons each day. About 850 tons of oxides of nitrogen combine with other ingredients to form an atmosphere which can be eye-irritating, ugly, and literally breath-taking. So far as primary pollutants in the Los Angeles area are concerned, many of them have been virtually eliminated, for this area has the strictest controls on industrial emissions and household sources of pollution to be found anywhere in the world.

Other sizable urban communities in the United States have similar problems, but in a less extreme form. Generally speaking, there is a significant but diminishing amount of particulate substance in the air. Secondary photochemical products are becoming noticeable during some periods and in some instances have become highly significant. Since no systematic data on the secondary pollutants have been collected and analyzed over a substantial period of time, one cannot know precisely what has been happening, but it is clear that this form of pollution has been rising rapidly.

FUTURE PROBLEMS

What can be said about the future direction of air pollution? Unfortunately, we must rely on the most general kind of indicators. Since 1940 U.S. use of energy has doubled and urban population has grown by a half. Rapid increases in these factors affecting air pollution appear inevitable. Recent projections made by Resources for the Future indicate that the United States may have a population of over 300 million by the end of the century and that more than three quarters of these people will live in urban areas. A striking increase in the use of energy is also projected. For example, it is forecast that in the twenty years from 1955 to 1975, the use of coal will increase by 75 per cent, the use of oil by over 85 per cent, and that of natural gas by over 100 per cent. What can be inferred from these projections? One inference is that unless efforts to control particulate pollution continue at a high level, the recent downtrend will be reversed. Another is that secondary pollution resulting from the combustion of fuels, primarily liquid and gaseous fuels, will continue to increase rapidly in the absence of intensified control efforts.

A rough idea of the costs that can be incurred—at least as they relate to the control of automobile fumes—is provided by some projections undertaken in California, a state which has pioneered in attempting to control automobile exhaust emissions. In 1960 the legislature set up the Motor Vehicle Pollution Control Board to review and pass on devices for controlling exhaust gases. In 1964 the Board approved four "afterburner" devices to help eliminate unburned hydrocarbons from auto exhausts. All 1966 cars sold in California must be equipped with an approved device of this type, and in a few years they will probably be mandatory on old cars as well. Several manufacturers have announced that most of the 1966 cars marketed in California will be equipped with an engine device which will meet the established standards without the need of an exhaust pipe mounted device. It has been estimated that the cost of automobile exhaust controls in California will be several hundred million and may be as high as a billion dollars.[5] While these controls will improve the situation as it exists today, it is questionable whether they are adequate for the future. It has been estimated for Los Angeles, for example, that if the pattern of automobile use continues, if the area's population continues to grow at its present rate, and given the present control standards, the automobile pollution problem will be as bad in a decade as it is now.

---

[5] Goldsmith (reference 6). The "built-in" devices may be capable of bringing the cost down somewhat.

A COMPARISON OF AIR AND WATER POLLUTION PROBLEMS

There are important parallels and contrasts between the effects and possible modes of management of water and air pollution.

1. In the United States and abroad, air pollution is heavily implicated as a factor affecting public health. Water pollution may be more costly in terms of non-human resources, but the current link of water pollution to public health problems on any large scale in this country is a matter of suspicion concerning chronic effects rather than of firm evidence. The somewhat stronger evidence on links between air pollution and health has been summarized by a former Surgeon General of the U.S. Public Health Service in part as follows:

a. Comparison of morbidity and mortality statistics with indices of air pollution suggests that communities with the heaviest air pollution loads tend to rank high in death rates from a number of diseases.

b. There is a significant correlation between air pollution and cancer of the esophagus and stomach, lung cancer, and arteriosclerotic disease.

Even so, the speculative character of these findings is striking. We are far from being able to trace specified causes and effects and relate them to the most efficient means of control. For example, while Los Angeles smog has been the subject of almost endless writing and a great deal of research, no one is quite sure what the eye-irritating agents in the smog actually are.

As in the case of water pollution, explicit evaluation of health effects of air pollution is not currently feasible, but valuable tests of the cost of achieving various levels of standards and their associated physical effects could be performed to aid the social decision process. Preferences for pollution-free air can perhaps be inferred from relative land values, expenditures for air purifiers, and commuting costs people are willing to incur to avoid polluted air.

2. As in the case of water pollution, a great many of the external costs imposed by air pollutants would appear to be rather

readily measurable, but no systematic measurement has yet been undertaken. These are, for example, soiling, corrosion, reduction in property values, and even agricultural losses. Crop damage from air pollution has been detected in many states. Damage claims have ranged from a slight reduction in crop yields to loss of entire farm enterprises. Some empirical investigations of these damages are now getting under way.

3. There are fewer means of dealing with air pollution than with water pollution. In part this is because it is easier for man to control hydrological events than meteorological events. In part it is because air is not delivered to users in pipes as water frequently is, so that it is only to a limited extent that polluted air is treatable before it is consumed. Therefore, we are in somewhat the same position in regard to polluted air as the fish are with polluted water. We live in it. Accordingly, control of air pollution is largely a matter of preventing pollutants from escaping from their source, eliminating the source, or of shifting location of the source or the recipient. Water pollution, on the other hand, is in general subject to a larger array of control measures. Nevertheless, both present intricate problems of devising optimal control systems.

In both cases we need to understand much better the role that location controls can play in optimal management. While there is some experience with this in air pollution, especially in the Ruhr area of Germany, in most cities industries and associated activities are now located in river valleys to take advantage of transportation facilities, but these locations are least satisfactory for dispersal of aerial wastes. Also, river bottom locations are peculiarly subject to flooding, the control of which represents one of our largest categories of public works investments. We must improve our ability to understand and plan for optimal location of activities in the urban complex in view of *all* the associated costs and benefits—public and private, internal and external.

4. Air pollution from fixed sources is usually much more localized than water pollution. As streams of wind carry the pollutants for any appreciable distance, dilution is ordinarily sufficient to mitigate their harmfulness. This contrasts with water

pollution where streams are like conduits, carrying persistent types of pollution farther and farther downstream. Thus, while air pollution certainly involves substantial external costs, it is more difficult to shift the burden completely to another geographical area. Accordingly, remedies, though costly, are much more clearly related to benefits within comparatively localized political jurisdictions. Even so, some students of the problem have felt that it could usefully be addressed in terms of regional air sheds analogous to watersheds. These air sheds of course do not necessarily correspond to any existing political jurisdictions. One comment along these lines is as follows: "We must learn to think about the finite but variable air supply of metropolitan regions and to plan our uses of air accordingly. It is possible to think, plan, measure and act upon the existences of air sheds in somewhat the same way as we are learning to consider entire river basins as units in the planning and conservation of water resources."[6]

The prevailing wind pattern and terrain in any given area of sufficient size determine to some extent the boundaries of an air shed which bear some resemblance to the boundaries of a watershed or river valley. On the west coast of California, where there is a prevailing westerly breeze, there exist several well-defined urban air sheds, one in the San Francisco Bay area and another in the Los Angeles area. Each is bounded by a rim of mountains or hills but is more or less open to the west.

Another boundary of an air shed is a ceiling which results from inhibition to vertical mixing due to stability of the air mass. Temperature normally decreases with height in the atmosphere. The change of temperature with height is called the lapse rate. The smaller the lapse rate, the greater the energy required to effect vertical exchange. When temperature increases with height (negative lapse rate) an inversion condition exists which tends to restrict vertical mixing. Shallow inversions may be produced nightly under clear skies and light wind conditions. If the vertical extent of the inversion is great enough, solar heating may not be able to break the inversion. While inversion conditions

[6] Goldsmith (reference 6).

are indeed important in severe air pollution episodes, some writing has tended to emphasize them to the exclusion of other equally important factors, particularly wind speed. Generally, as we all know, the higher the wind speed the greater the dispersion of air-borne materials.

The notion of an air shed may be a useful concept for analysis and control of air pollution, but the problems in its use should not be minimized. In the case of water pollution, the stochastic character of streamflow presents difficulties in measuring associated costs and in designing and operating optimum systems for water quality control. The air shed adds more dimensions to this problem. It may be likened to a stream which varies its course rapidly (within defined boundaries), changes specific gravity, and from time to time decides to flow uphill. We must learn to understand and, at least in a probabilistic sense, forecast these phenomena.

5. To the extent that air sheds are definable, air shed authorities or compacts or districts are conceivable and may be useful administrative devices. There is some precedent here, for example, in the formation of the San Francisco Bay area air pollution control district. In Germany an important part of the work of the *Siedlungsverband* (Land Planning Authority) is to deal with problems of air pollution. The primary means used in Germany is the control of location of industrial activities. Efforts of this kind present useful laboratories for studying the costs and effectiveness of various approaches.

6. As in the case of water pollution, there may be some administrative and regulatory alternatives to standards which demand serious consideration, for example, some variety of air pollution charge or tax. This would be levied on the theory that use of a congested facility, air, should be reduced by putting a price on its use. Such a tax would be based on some measure of pollutants discharged at the source and could be weighted according to location of the source, the external costs of specific pollutants, timing of releases in relation to peak loads of air congestion, wind direction, etc.

THE SPECIAL PROBLEM OF CO_2

We cannot end our discussion of air pollution without mentioning one other problem whose possible implications are vast. This is the accumulation of CO_2 (carbon dioxide) in the air due to the combustion of fossil fuels. Within a comparatively few years man is oxidizing (through burning) carbonaceous materials which have accumulated through geologic time. The result has been a substantial increase in the CO_2 content of the air.[7] If the use of fossil fuels continues to climb commensurately with the growth of economic activity the CO_2 in the atmosphere could grow by more than half over its present level by the end of the century. In the very long run, the atmospheric CO_2 must be in equilibrium with that contained in water reservoirs (principally the oceans). Therefore, part of the addition to the atmosphere will be absorbed into the water. It is thought, however, that this process would take thousands of years to restore equilibrium if CO_2 increases as estimated.

What is the significance of all this for man? No one really knows. It is known that atmospheric CO_2 is one of the substances which helps to retain the heat of the sun in the atmosphere and thus may be an important factor in the earth's climate. Some scientists believe that measurable increases in temperature have already occurred as a consequence of the CO_2 build-up. Small temperature changes, say an increase of one degree on the average, have profound effects on the world's climate. While few, if any, scientists working on air pollution are willing to forecast the dire effects sometimes foreseen in the popular press, all are concerned. Should effects on climate and other aspects of the human environment turn out to be adverse, we would face a problem of control on a global scale that might require massive efforts to reduce our dependency on fossil fuels. About all one can say at this point is that it is urgently important that we observe the situation closely and endeavor to learn more about the role of CO_2 in the determination of climate.

[7] See *Implications of Rising Carbon Dioxide Content of the Atmosphere* (New York: Conservation Foundation, 1963).

Some Selected References on Air Pollution

1. *Air Over Cities.* U.S. Department of Health, Education, and Welfare, Public Health Service, Taft Sanitary Engineering Center, Cincinnati, 1961.
2. *Air Pollution Control.* Hearings before the Special Subcommittee on Air and Water Pollution of the Senate Committee on Public Works, 88th Congress, 1st Session. Washington: U.S. Government Printing Office, 1963.
3. *Clean Air.* Hearings before the Special Subcommittee on Air and Water Pollution of the Senate Committee on Public Works, 88th Congress, 2nd Session. Washington: U.S. Government Printing Office, 1964, parts 1 & 2.
4. Fair, Gordon M. "New Factors in Man's Management of His Environment," Chadwick Lecture delivered in the Royal Hall, Harrogate (England), on April 28, 1959, in conjunction with the Health Congress of the Royal Society of Health.
5. Gaffney, M. Mason. "Economic Analysis and Air Conservation," to appear in Report of Air Conservation Commission to American Association for the Advancement of Science, in press.
6. Goldsmith, John R. "Urban Air Conservation," *Bulletin of the Atomic Scientists*, November 1961.

CHAPTER IV

THE USE OF CHEMICALS
AS PESTICIDES

Chemicals are so much a part of the fabric of modern society that, whether deliberately sought or not, they permeate all economic sectors, including households. Some of their effects may in some cases be neutral or even favorable to the well-being of men, but concern is increasing over the possibility of adverse effects on men, domestic and wild animals, and perhaps the whole ecology of a region. Moreover, the mere fact that uncertainty exists may produce anxieties which themselves generate harmful effects. There is clear need to find out what may be the external diseconomies associated with the use of pesticides.

Some aspects of the problems in this area are closely related to those that have been discussed in connection with water and air pollution. Water and air were selected as useful categories for discussion in Chapters II and III because, being carriers of a variety of pollutants, not the least among which are chemical pollutants, they form an appropriate focus for analysis and policy. Here we examine the pollutant chemicals themselves, for they are distributed in the environment by a variety of media which include water and air.

Perhaps it is owing to the widespread use of DDT in recent years that people in general have become acquainted with a biochemical fact: that portions of some chemicals used for insecticides and other purposes are involuntarily accumulated in the human body. The individual has only limited power to avoid exposure to these chemicals. True, he can shun those occupations or activities that require their direct handling. A few stores specialize in foods that have been grown and processed without the intentional use of man-made chemicals. But most of us have little effective choice. We drink water without question as it comes from the tap. Food is purchased in the trust that the regulatory agencies have seen to it that residues of these potentially harmful substances are below harmful levels. The limitations on any individual attempt to avoid such substances is strikingly suggested by a two-year-old report of the U.S. Fish and Wildlife Service, indicating that duck eggs in a sample collected in northern Canada, 500 miles north of any known application of insecticide, contained an average of 2.2 ppm DDT.[1] The channels by which DDT has reached these eggs are not well understood. DDT and probably some other pesticides apparently can be found in most places on the earth—land or water—although local concentrations vary greatly. The fact that pesticides often are applied from planes is in itself sufficient to insure universal dispersion of these substances, but there are other means of dispersion. Water is an important source of movement and dispersion, as is also the concentration of pesticides by various organisms and their subsequent progress through food chains.

Recent decades have brought two developments which are relevant to appraisal of the pesticide problem. First, their use has increased enormously. Second, this increase reflects a major shift in the chemicals used, for it is the net result of a larger use of a number of new chemicals with which we perforce have had little experience, and a considerably smaller use of the well-tried pesticides. Before World War II pesticides were made up mainly of inorganic substances, such as copper sulfate, arsenate of lead, calcium arsenate, etc., many of which have a long history of use. Beginning with the development of DDT, however, the use of chlorinated hydrocarbons increased greatly. This category includes such pesticides as dieldrin, aldrin, endrin, toxaphene, lindane, and chlordane, as well as the herbicides 2,4–D, and 2,4,5–T. Also brought into production were organic phosphorous compounds, among which are parathion and malathion. Generally

---

[1] Reference 9 at p. 47. See Selected References at end of this chapter, p. 52.

speaking, the organic phosphorous compounds are less persistent than the chlorinated hydrocarbons. Persistence, of course, is one of the main reasons for the external effects of pesticides, for desirable as it may be for some uses of the chemical, it insures transmittal of the substance to humans if a channel is available.

In the United States, the total weight of pesticide production in 1960 was one and one-half that of 1950 and three times that of 1939.[2] "Tons produced" is not a satisfactory index of effectiveness when the composition of output changes as much as it has with pesticides. However, since effectiveness per ton is greater for the new than for the old pesticides, it is clear that in terms of effectiveness the country's output of pesticides has increased enormously.

Comparable data on use of pesticides in the United States are not available for any extended period, but it is clear that there have been important divergences in the consumption trends of various pesticides and herbicides. While the use of DDT[3] has remained approximately constant over the ten-year period from 1951 to 1962, consumption of several inorganic poisons dropped radically. Use of lead arsenate declined by almost 75 per cent over the eleven-year period before 1962. The use of copper sulfate declined by about a third over the same span of time, and the consumption of calcium arsenate at the end of this period was little more than a tenth of what it was at the beginning. Use of the organic aldrin-toxaphene group, on the other hand, grew enormously, so much so that its poundage exceeded by a fifth that of DDT at the end of the period. In terms of weight, the leading categories in 1961–62 were the aldrin-toxaphene group, copper sulfate, DDT, and 2,4–D.

All this has resulted in much more land being treated with pesticides; but most of it is comparatively high-value land. The extent to which different types of land are treated varies greatly, a fact well illustrated by some estimates of acreages treated with insecticides made by the Entomological Society of America.

[2] We rely here on data compiled by Headley and Lewis in reference 3.
[3] Strictly speaking, domestic disappearance. The data are from *ibid.*

TABLE 2. LAND TREATED WITH INSECTICIDES IN THE 48 CONTIGUOUS STATES, 1962

Type of land	Total acres (*millions*)		Per cent treated
Urban or built-up	53		28
Cropland and cropland pasture	457		15
Fruits, nuts		3	80
Cotton		16	75
Vegetables		4	50
Grains		217	15
All other		217	9
Desert, swamp, dunes, and wildland	77		3.2
Forest	640		.28
Grassland	630		.25
Other	78		—
Total—48 states	1,935		4.6

Source: See reference 9 at p. 3.

Acreage treated with all pesticides—i.e., fungicides, herbicides, and insecticides—must naturally be larger than those shown in Table 2, which are estimates based on insecticide treatment only. Taking farmland alone, for example, the U.S. Department of Agriculture has estimated that 55 million acres of farmland were treated for weed control in 1958 as compared with 37 million for insect and disease control. The total farm acreage treated for all purposes is less than the sum of these two figures because some land is treated for both purposes, but the total for that year was considerably more than the 55 million acres.

Farm acreage treated for insect and disease control increased by 28 per cent in the six years from 1952 to 1958. Acreage treated for weed control increased by 78 per cent over the same period. Some land is treated several times during a season, of course, especially for insect control. Land growing fruit and nut trees receives the largest number of treatments for insect and disease control—5 in 1958 as compared with an average 2.4 treatments for other types of land treated.[4]

[4] Strickler and Hinson (reference 7), p. 9.

EFFECTS OF PESTICIDES

Some of the more obvious gains from the use of pesticides have been trumpeted so loudly and so long that discussion is hardly needed. Data are abundant which demonstrate that pesticides in many situations vastly increase crop yields and improve quality as compared with crops grown without their use. Apples and other fruits, cotton, and potatoes are outstanding examples of such crops.

But there are more subtle gains. Reduction of fluctuation in crop yields—or, more precisely, reduction of the frequency of years with very low yields—has many effects which add up to a reduction in the cost of producing food. Financial risk is reduced, which in turn makes it possible for farms with limited access to capital to use low-cost methods of production requiring more capital. Reduction of crop-yield fluctuations has been one of the elements in the increase in size of farm that has taken place over the last few decades.[5]

From some points of view, the effects of pesticides on human health throughout the world have been even more important than the effects on crop yields. Large reductions in the incidence of malaria and some other diseases were effected during and after World War II, mainly through the use of DDT to control mosquitoes and other carriers of these diseases. The increase in both potential and actual human welfare has been enormous. Length of life has been increased and debility has been decreased, accompanied by the dubious blessing of very rapid increases in population. In the United States, however, the favorable effects of pesticides on health have been far less spectacular, mainly because the incidence of diseases with carriers against which pesticides are effective was much lower to begin with.

On the debit side, pesticides present obvious acute dangers, for most of them are toxic to humans as well as to pests. The main acute dangers seem to be around the site of use. The United

---

[5] See Headley and Lewis (reference 3), p. 88, for a more detailed discussion of these matters.

States suffers some 150 deaths a year from acute poisoning, and about half of these involve children.[6] The number of non-fatal poisonings is not known, partly because of difficulties of diagnosis, but it may be in the tens of thousands judging by the 4,000 cases known to have occurred in California in 1960.[7] While the acute dangers to humans from the use of pesticides are serious and warrant careful attention, they are a secondary part of the current controversy over the use of pesticides.

This controversy centers around, first, the largely unknown long-term effects on humans from prolonged exposure to pesticides and, second, the acute effects of pesticides on wildlife. As to human exposure, a major source of concern is the fact that the individual cannot effectively avoid or control his exposure. Everyone is subject to more or less the same risk. The amount of exposure is the result of a complex set of forces involving natural processes, the pesticides available and practices followed in their use, and public regulation.

It is well established that pesticides do get into the human body. Analyses of total diets, prepared as they are in the home, show that commonly used pesticides are present in the foods we eat, although usually below official maxima.[8] Whether the quantity of pesticides reaching humans will have adverse long-term effects is not yet known, for our exposure to the pesticides used during and after World War II has, after all, not been very long. But the problem is complicated by the rapidity with which new pesticides are being introduced.

Recent studies have shown that DDT now forms about twelve parts per million of the fatty tissue of U.S. residents.[9] The proportion does not appear to have increased over the last decade but, while studies have been made of DDT's biochemistry and of its effects on mammals, including humans, we still cannot be sure

[6] These deaths are about three times the annual deaths from floods. The annual cost of flood protection, which is justified on the argument that it saves lives, is in the millions of dollars. This raises the interesting question whether total lives saved would be increased by transferring some money from flood protection to attempts to reduce deaths from pesticides.

[7] See reference 6 at p. 9.

[8] See Fishbach (reference 2), p. 62.

[9] From Report (reference 6), p. 6.

of its long-term effects. Our concern is not only with possible pathological effects—some pesticides, for example, may produce cancer at concentrations found in humans—but also with possibilities of genetic damage. The answers to these questions may never be known, for there are so many forces at work that it will always be very hard to be sure what caused a particular effect.

As to the other main source of controversy—the acute effects of pesticides on wildlife—in specific cases they have been most severe. Even though, so far as we know, no widespread adverse effect on the over-all wildlife population has yet been established, there is no doubt that at certain locations and for unknown periods of time some bird populations have been greatly reduced. Extensive fish kills have been traced to pesticides which, in many cases, had been applied at conventional levels. Entirely apart from the warnings these incidents raise for human health and ecological well-being, large numbers of people are concerned with what is happening to the birds, beasts, and fish. Millions hunt and fish, and millions more derive enjoyment from the presence of wildlife in nearby areas which, more often than not, are the very urban and agricultural areas in which the use of pesticides is concentrated.

PRESENT REGULATION

When a pesticide is not to be used on a food crop, the U.S. Department of Agriculture will register it for use if it is not "injurious to man, vertebrate animals, or vegetation, except weeds," provided it is used in accordance with instructions on the label.[10] When a pesticide is to be used on a food crop, the same registration criteria apply if it leaves no residue on the plant.[11] If a residue does remain on the food crop, then a "residue tolerance" must be established by the Food and Drug Administration before registration will be granted. The maker of the pesticide must

[10] P.L. 104, 80th Congress, 1st Session, Sec. 2u (2) (g).
[11] In practice, this has to mean "almost no residue" if methods of measurement are sensitive enough.

present experimental data on the basis of which a tolerance level can be established. Tolerance levels are said to be commonly set at 1/100th of the level at which harmful effects are observed in the most sensitive type of animal tested.[12]

After these initial steps, the Food and Drug Administration inspects about 1 per cent of the food products moving in interstate commerce to detect cases where tolerance levels have been exceeded.[13] Some 2 to 3 per cent of the domestic shipments inspected have contained illegal pesticide residues during the last couple of years. This raises the interesting question of the extent to which the uninspected shipments containing illegal residues are responsible for the pesticides which get into humans. Since 1954, the maker of the pesticide has been required to provide a feasible method for administering the tolerance level regulations.

NEXT STEPS

The situation described above has produced an intense controversy. The diversity and range of opinions and the vehemence with which they have been expressed has been little short of astounding. Since first it was realized that many of the new chemicals were not only spectacularly successful in killing their targets, but also produced spectacular unwanted external effects, the suspicion has grown that the new pesticides might have serious effects on humans and on their environment that would not be detected until serious and irreparable damage had been done. Beyond doubt, the outstanding articulation of their actual and possible dangers was the late Rachel Carson's *Silent Spring*.

One of the interesting aspects of this controversy is the frequency with which a representative of discipline A asserts that a member of discipline B is making a serious error because he is unaware of some elementary proposition of the other discipline. It has been said, for example, that highway engineers don't know

---

[12] Hearings (reference 10), p. 85.
[13] *Ibid.*, p. 191.

that ragweed is a pioneer; that chemists don't realize that a simple environment is unstable; that "naturalists" don't understand that all substances get dispersed, that all substances are dangerous if ingested beyond certain levels; and so on. Possibly there is some truth in all of these allegations of ignorance. It is certain that an understanding of the effects of pesticides involves many disciplines. Hence one necessary ingredient of progress toward resolution of the problem is a continuation of controversy in order that interested parties may learn about the relevant facts and principles each discipline has to offer.

In attempting to fill the enormous gaps in our knowledge, three objectives should be kept in mind: first, a better understanding of the adverse effects of pesticides, especially chronic effects on humans; second, a better understanding of the economic and other aspects of pesticide use; and third, the development of pesticide controls which will reduce the risk of damage to humans and wildlife.

Adverse Effects of Pesticides. A considerable amount of data exists on the effects of pesticides on wildlife. The various investigatory programs which have produced this information need to be continued. Up to now, however, it has not been possible to sum up the findings of the investigations so as to show whether the "total" of the effects is increasing or decreasing through time. We may be at the point where this can be done area by area. For example, an annual sampling of the pesticide content of the tissue of various types of wildlife would be useful, especially if analyzed in conjunction with various types of data on pesticide use in the same areas, e.g., types and quantities of pesticide used, mode of application, etc.

When we turn to the possible chronic effects of pesticides on humans, we find that information is very bare indeed. But there seems no good reason why these effects cannot be studied profitably together with the study of other substances to which humans are subjected in the course of modern life, such as air and water pollutants and food additives. The techniques and the disciplines required for studying all of these matters are similar.

The Economics and Methods of Pesticide Use. Even though we are uncertain about the extent of the external or side effects of pesticide use, it is possible to reduce these effects by a careful choice of methods and rates of application. The relevant question is not whether the total favorable effects outweigh the unfavorable.[14] Unfortunately, this is a view which seems to underlie much of the current discussion of the pesticide problem and even much of the research on the economic benefits of pesticides. Where this view is held, the focus of investigation often seems to have been on the effect of *eliminating* use of the pesticide. The question, rather, is how to reduce adverse effects substantially without giving up all of the benefits. To make these finer choices, more subtle questions should be asked in our research. For example, what would be the effects of various size reductions in application rates on yields, other production costs, *and* on unwanted transmission costs? How would these variables be affected by changes in application methods? It may prove possible to reduce unwanted transmission substantially by comparatively small changes in application rates and techniques with only a small increase in production costs.

To build up information of this sort, a better understanding of the routes and processes by which pesticides get to humans and to wildlife is needed. Study of pesticide transmission is under way and should be continued.[15] The monitoring programs now in effect—pesticide content of human diet; inspection of food shipments, pesticide content of wildlife—are essential and probably need to be expanded. We cannot deal with any hazard, known or suspected, without the factual information provided by such investigations.

The Array of Pest Control Methods. The adverse effects of pesticides, whatever their precise nature, also can be reduced by choosing less dangerous methods of control as well as by the way

---

[14] It may come as a surprise to some that the following words were written by Rachel Carson: "It is not my contention that chemical insecticides must never be used." See reference 1 at p. 22.

[15] The U.S. Department of Health, Education, and Welfare recently (early 1964) made a sizable grant to Rutgers University for the study of such problems.

in which a given method is used. Which methods of control are less dangerous, especially for chronic effects on humans? This is not a simple question, but still it seems to us that research on methods, both economic and technical, could well emphasize: (1) less persistent toxicants, (2) toxicants with more specific effects, and (3) methods of control other than toxicants (sometimes called "biological" controls).

The advantages to be gained by shifting use away from the most persistent toxicants need to be evaluated very carefully—quantitatively so far as this is possible. The quality of persistence is desirable in many applications, of course, for it permits a smaller number of applications. Nevertheless, one of the ways for society to buy lower levels of, say, DDT in the human body and elsewhere is to use less of it, substituting pesticides which are more rapidly reduced to harmless compounds both in and outside the human body.

Another way to reduce the exposure of humans and other organisms to potentially damaging pesticides is to develop and use compounds that are more specific in their effect, that is, compounds which affect a smaller range of different organisms. This is more easily said than done, as is obvious from the fact that many of the most effective pesticides are extremely toxic to man when they get into his body as well as to their intended targets. Still, the art of developing new pesticides has advanced considerably, so much so that it is not fanciful to ask that pesticides be developed which have less dangerous effects on organisms other than the target.

While no toxicant is likely to affect only its target, there are methods for dealing with pests which affect only the target, except, of course, for the ecological repercussions resulting from the lower pest population. There are several such methods, some as old as agriculture and some of recent development. The development of resistant varieties has been an important defensive weapon against many kinds of pests. It is well known, for example, that efforts to develop rust-resistant varieties of wheat have been very successful, but continual effort to find hardy, disease-resistant varieties is a necessary part of all agriculture, partly because nature develops new pests and new ailments. Resistant varieties cannot be found for every pest, at least not within reasonable periods of time, but the search is successful enough of the time to warrant continued and perhaps expanded expenditure on such efforts.

Parasites or predators may be and have been used to combat pests. According to the President's Science Advisory Committee Panel on the Use of Pesticides[16] over 500 insect enemies have been imported of which some 36 have been successful to varying degrees. This may seem to be a rather low score, but perhaps it is not. An assessment of the costs and benefits of these attempts is much needed, for the net benefits may have been great enough to warrant expanded effort on such controls in the future.

There are some comparatively new biological controls, which by their very nature are completely specific. One consists in the use of attractants together with a toxicant, for example, sexual attractants operating by odor. Some extremely powerful attractants for a few insects have been developed and used successfully. Lures have played an important part in identifying the areas which are infested with the gypsy moth, the Mediterranean fruit fly, the oriental fruit fly, the melon fly, the Mexican fruit fly, and the European chafer.[17]

Another completely specific biological control is to raise and release large numbers of male insects that have been sterilized but are otherwise sexually competent. The method has been used to control the screwworm fly in Florida and other parts of the South and may prove to be useful on a much wider scale.

CHOICES AND THEIR IMPLEMENTATION

The discussion to this point has emphasized the need for quantitative information on all the aspects of the pesticide problem and has stressed the significance of uncertainty about the effects

[16] See reference 6 at p. 14.
[17] See reference 4 for a discussion of attractants.

of pesticides for their use. So far, however, the adequacy of existing legislation and institutions to bring about any change in pesticide use has not been explored. Suppose we decided, as a society, that human and wildlife exposure to pesticides should be reduced. What levers could be pulled, if any? Could this be done within existing legislation and practices, or would new law and procedure be required?

The answers to these and similar questions are far from clear to us. Indeed, it is our feeling that hardly any serious and expert attention has been given these questions in the discussion since World War II. The question of legislative adequacy seems to have been examined only within the context of the type of regulation we now have, granted the importance of the changes in legislation and practice that have been made within this framework.

To get at the problem of institutional adequacy, we shall discuss three possible changes from present pesticide use that society might decide to encourage, and consider whether existing institutions could bring about such change.

1. *More Careful Use of Pesticides Now in Use.* Insofar as improper use leaves illegal residues on interstate shipments of food, existing regulation could be used to discourage improper use. The 1 percent or so of interstate shipments that is now inspected for residues, could be raised easily. Residues on intrastate shipments of foods are controlled in some states but, on the whole, state regulation of residues is less stringent than that of the federal government.

Where improper use affecting humans and wildlife does not leave illegal residues on interstate food shipments, the federal government does not regulate use at present and perhaps would have no constitutional basis for doing so. State governments clearly have the power to regulate such matters and would be the main instrument for improvement of present practice. It seems reasonably clear that existing state regulation permits a substantial amount of misuse of pesticides, although stringency of regulation varies greatly among the states. Further, we suspect

that existing *types* of regulation could not go very far in eliminating misuse. The level of care now exercised is probably at-
tributable to factors other than existing regulations—the user's
sense of responsibility and the standards suggested by makers of
pesticides.

Consideration of the type of regulation or institution needed to
reduce misuse emphasizes once again the importance of having
some quantitative information on the location and types of misuse and on routes followed by pesticides to humans and wildlife.

2. *Encourage the Use of Less Persistent and More Specific
Toxicants.* The federal government clearly has the power to
move its own control programs toward the use of less persistent
and more specific toxicants. These are administered mainly by
the Department of Agriculture, including the Forest Service,
and the Department of the Interior. For example, in September
1964 the Secretary of the Interior issued an order designed to
minimize hazards to humans and wildlife in pesticide applications
by agencies of the Department. An appraisal of the effectiveness
of the regulation should be made after it has been in effect for
a time.

The adequacy of the federal government's power to encourage
private businesses and individuals to use less persistent and more
specific pesticides is not so clear. Present legislation imposes re-
strictions on the manufacturer and, in some cases, on the shipper
of food products: (1) the pesticide must meet certain standards
before what is in effect a license for sale will be granted; (2)
use by growers of food products is partially and indirectly regulated in that residues on interstate shipments may not exceed
official standards. As it stands, however, this legislation is not
very suitable for encouraging use of less persistent and more
specific toxicants, although new criteria for residue standards
could be used to achieve this objective in the case of food crops.

The states have the power to encourage a shift in the types of
pesticides used, but little consideration seems to have been given
to the procedures or type of regulation that would be most suit-

able. The problems here are analogous to those of water and air pollution, with the same array of possibilities for control. The problem of controlling pesticides has its own peculiarities, however, the principal one being the very great geographical dispersion of the activity and the complexity of the routes by which they are transmitted to humans and wildlife.

Among the possibilities to be considered is the use of taxes to encourage a shift in pesticides used. Would it be desirable to tax certain uses of persistent toxicants, assuming a reduction in exposure has been adopted as an objective of public policy? If it were known, for example, that certain uses produce no external effects, they should not be taxed. But if uses were not thought to differ very much in their external effects, a tax on all use or on the production of the toxicant would achieve a reduction in its use, especially in those uses where effective substitutes are available.

3. *Encourage the Use of "Biological" Control of Pests.* The encouragement of greater use of biological controls presents different problems, in that their use will more often involve public activity. The search for resistant varieties involves public research programs, although there is also much private research. The other biological control possibilities, however, often require so large a scale of operation or diffuse benefits so widely that their use by comparatively small economic units is impractical. Perhaps the use of attractants is something of an exception, at least in certain cases, as they would be used to lower expenditure on a toxicant and its application, but predator and parasite programs and sterilization programs would seem more often to require public operation.

Agencies and programs for the development and use of biological controls are in operation and have been for many years. The only obstacles to the increased use of biological controls are money for research and application and the reluctance of nature to reveal her secrets. As new possibilities are found, it is quite likely that they will be used.

PROSPECTS

The way we use pesticides now has produced demonstrated adverse effects on wildlife in many instances and demonstrated acute effects on substantial numbers of humans. Chronic adverse effects on the general population from exposures actually encountered have not yet been demonstrated, but some investigators feel they may turn out to be important.

The prospects for advancing our understanding beyond this stage are not encouraging. The problem of chronic effects on humans seems especially difficult, for the situation is such as to produce rapid change in both pests and pesticides. Pests do evolve "around" pesticides, as has been demonstrated many times. This necessitates a shift to different or new pesticides, a shift which is speeded by the rapid rate with which new compounds are developed. Thus, the target in investigations of chronic effects is continually shifting. The problem is made even more difficult by the fact that experiment on humans takes a long time, is costly, and often is impractical because of the risks involved.

The problem of finding out more about the effects of pesticides presents an interesting and important contrast to the smoking problem. The fact that consumption is involuntary for pesticides while it is voluntary for cigarettes means that statistical study of the consumption effects of the chemicals is much more difficult than for cigarettes. In the case of cigarettes only a part of the population has been consuming them. This has given us the opportunity to compare the condition of groups of persons who differ only in that part of them smoke cigarettes and part of them do not. Granted that there are distinct limitations on the certainty of the knowledge which can be extracted from the study of statistical data involving smokers and non-smokers, these data leave us in an immeasurably better position to gauge health and other effects than we are with pesticides. All of the population consume pesticides in some measure. It is difficult, therefore, if not impossible, to find two groups of people who are alike in relevant respects except for their consumption of these chemicals.

To find a group of people that does not consume them we must go, unfortunately, to cultures that differ from ours in many respects, some of which will be relevant to the presence or absence of the very effects that may be influenced by the consumption of the chemicals. The prospects for developing a sure understanding of long-run effects are dim, indeed. Finally, if our legislators should decide that the lower damage and insurance against chronic effects warrant closer control of the use of certain pesticides even though some costs may be increased, the type of regulation we now have perhaps would be quite inadequate to the task.

The problems posed by pesticides are similar to those posed by many other substances peculiar to the modern world. We have no choice but to try to amass relevant facts and to try to reach agreement on courses of action in a way which takes explicit account of the fact of our glaring ignorance. It would be well to face directly the question of how much we are willing to pay in increased food costs for a reduction in the magnitude of adverse effects of unknown but possibly sizable magnitude.

Some Selected References on Pesticides

1. Carson, Rachel. *Silent Spring*. New York: Crest Book, 1964.
2. Fishbach, Henry. "Problems Stemming From The Refinement of Analytical Methods," in *New Developments and Problems in the Use of Pesticides*, Publication 1082. Washington: National Academy of Sciences-National Research Council, 1963, p. 62.
3. Headley, J. C. and Lewis, J. N. *The Pesticide Problem: An Economic Approach to Public Policy*. University of Illinois, Department of Agricultural Economics, 1964 (mimeo).
4. Jacobson, Martin and Beroza, Morton. "Insect Attractants," *Scientific American*, August 1964, p. 20.
5. National Academy of Sciences-National Research Council. *Pest Control and Wildlife Relationships: Part I, Evaluation of Pesticide-Wildlife Problems; Part II, Policy and Procedures for Pest Control; Part III, Research Needs*. Publications 920-A and 920-B (1962) and 920-C (1963), Washington.
6. Report of the President's Science Advisory Committee. *Use of Pesticides*. Washington, May 15, 1963.
7. Strickler, Paul E. and Hinson, William C. "Extent of Spraying and Dusting on Farms, 1958 with Comparisons," *Statistical Bulletin* No. 314, U.S. Department of Agriculture, Economic Research Service. Washington, May 1962.
8. U.S. Department of Agriculture, *Documentary Evidence of Benefits Derived from the Use of Pesticides in Agriculture*. Report of Information Provided by the Entomology Research, Crops Research, Plant Pest Control and Animal Disease Eradication Divisions of the Agricultural Research Service; the Market Quality Division of the Agricultural Marketing Service and the Division of Forest Pest Control, Forest Service. Washington, April 2, 1963 (unpublished).
9. U.S. Fish and Wildlife Service. *Pesticide-Wildlife Studies*, U.S. Department of the Interior, Circular 167. Washington, June 1963.
10. U.S. Senate, Subcommittee on Reorganization and International Organizations of the Committee on Government Operations. "Inter-Agency Coordination in Environmental Hazards (Pesticides)." 88th Congress, 1st Session. Washington: U.S. Government Printing Office, 1964.

CHAPTER V

THE PHYSICAL ENVIRONMENT
OF URBAN PLACES

Certain costs resulting from noise, congestion, dirt, and foul air are associated with the benefits of the compact habitation afforded by urban areas. It is a mistake, however, to think of these problems as being characteristic solely of contemporary times. As in the other areas we have reviewed, conflicting trends—some apparently favorable and some unfavorable—characterize urban environment. Some aspects of air and water sanitation in urbanized regions have improved markedly in recent decades; other aspects of the urban physical environment have changed also, and not necessarily for the worse. The following description of London in 1890 may help to illustrate the point:

A more assertive mark of the horse was the mud* (*a euphemism) that, despite the activities of a numerous corps of red-jacketed boys who dodged among wheels and hoofs with pan and brush in service to iron bins at the pavement-edge, either flooded the streets with churnings of "pea soup" that at times collected in pools overbrimming the kerbs, and at others covered the road-surface as with axle grease or bran-laden dust to the distraction of the wayfarer. In the first case, the swift moving hansom or gig would fling sheets of such soup—where not intercepted by trousers or skirts—completely across the pavement, so that the frontages of the Strand throughout its length had an eighteen-inch plinth of mud-parge thus imposed on it. The pea-soup condition was met by wheeled "mud-carts" each attended by two ladlers clothed as for Icelandic seas in thigh boots, oilskins collared to the chin, and sou'westers sealing in the back of the neck. Splash Ho! The foot passenger now gets the mud in his eye! The axle grease condition was met by horse-mechanized brushes and travelers in the small hours found fire hoses washing away the residues. . . .

And after the mud the noise, which, again endowed by the horse, surged like a mighty heart-beat in the central districts of London's life. It was a thing beyond all imaginings. The streets of workaday London were uniformly paved in "granite" sets . . . and the hammering of a multitude of iron-shod hairy heels upon [them], the deafening, side-drum tatoo of tyred wheels jarring from the apex of one set to the next, like sticks dragging along a fence; the creaking and groaning and chirping and rattling of vehicles, light and heavy, thus maltreated; the jangling of chain harness and the clanging or jingling of every other conceivable thing else, augmented by the shrieking and bellowings called for from those of God's creatures who desired to impart information or proffer a request vocally—raised a din that . . . is beyond conception. It was not any such paltry thing as noise. It was an immensity of sound. . . .[1]

The advent of the internal combustion engine, of course, drastically altered the character of urban areas everywhere, a process that is continuing at a rapid pace. Before investigating some of the problems that change has brought into being, let us look briefly at the role of urban areas in the United States today.

Although urban space takes up substantially less than 1 per cent of the nation's area, it houses three out of every four people in the country and produces well over four-fifths of the nation's economic output. In terms of land value, as much as 80 per cent is found in this minuscule part of the country's land surface. This massive concentration suggests the critical importance of urban efficiency to the national product, as well as the possibly huge social diseconomy which may occur as the result of failures to achieve optimum urban environmental quality.

[1] H. B. Creswell, *Architectural Review*, December 1958. Quoted by Jacobs (reference 4). See Selected References at end of this chapter, p. 64.

EFFECTS OF CHANGES
IN TRANSPORTATION COSTS

To an amazing degree, changes in the physical organization of the urban environment appear to have been a consequence of changes in transportation costs. In analyzing these effects, public costs (expenditures of funds by public bodies for the construction, operation, and maintenance of transportation facilities, and the costs imposed on other road users by a driver making an additional trip on a congested road) are to be distinguished from private costs (out-of-pocket money and time costs to the individual transportation user), because they measure different things and have different influences. Private costs influence the trip-making and location behavior of persons, while public costs bear upon the over-all performance of the total transportation system. In combination, these costs have a tremendous influence on the spatial organization of an urban region.

Public investment in transportation systems tends to reduce the private time or money costs of movement and thereby the costs of those economic linkages which take place through the movement of goods and persons. Much of the tight concentration of urban activities around a dense urban core can be explained by the economies that existed under earlier conditions when transportation costs were relatively high and there were substantial locational differentials in the cost of transporting materials and persons.

That things have changed is dramatically illustrated by comparing the spatial organization of the auto-age cities, such as Los Angeles, with their predecessors, such as Boston. Urban concentration—the great piling up of capital structures at the region's center tapering off dramatically as one moves toward the periphery—seems to be subsiding rapidly. For centrally located activities which find themselves functioning in an increasingly high private-cost part of the region, the lower transportation and land costs of outlying locations are appealing alternatives where new investment is involved. Retailing and manufacturing are already moving to the suburbs, and service industries are rapidly following. The result of this is the demise of the centrally articulated classical city. In its place is growing a loosely knit, weakly centered, low-density urban region spread over a wide hinterland. Sharply reduced private transportation costs outside the center make land or space even less a scarce good to be husbanded. The central city is less and less a focus for the economic and cultural life of the community.

Some have found this a melancholy prospect. Their view is that the great positive values of an urban civilization have stemmed from its compactness, from the concentrated variety that a Manhattan typifies, not from the monotonous homogeneity which middle-class suburban dispersion has produced. They feel that the mental stimulation offered by urban civilization derives from the contrast of city and countryside, that the sense of humanity it breeds stems from its ability to provide environments which will nurture many sides of the human spirit.[2]

This is a point of view that rests heavily on at least a vague notion of external economies. Whatever its merits may be, it is extremely difficult to marshal evidence bearing on its validity. It does appear to be true that in the United States it has been the very large cities that have achieved a degree of individuality and character and have provided a home for the arts as a living and growing part of human existence.

PUBLIC VS. PRIVATE TRANSPORTATION COSTS

Even if one accepts these propositions as having some merit, it may well be argued that the very structuring of our urban areas represents a desirable adaption to human demands and changing technology.[3] Before accepting this, however, one might wish to

---

[2] The three preceding paragraphs are drawn largely from Wingo (reference 7). See Cook in reference 2 at pp. 87 ff., for an argument that the density and rapidity of change in the urban environment are essential conditions for a high rate of cultural innovations.

[3] This appears to be implicit in Vernon (reference 6).

examine whether or not dispersion has been strongly abetted by the fact that decision makers were able to neglect certain public costs of their decisions. In other words, were they able to impose certain costs of dispersion on other parties whether they desire dispersion or not?

This certainly appears to be true of transportation. Public investment in outlying transportation has sharply reduced private transportation costs in suburban areas and dissipated many of the economic advantages of central location. The current strategy of constructing high-volume, high-speed radial freeways, articulated by sets of beltways or circumferentials, will amplify these effects.

Perhaps more importantly, we have not worked out an effective system of levying the external costs of automobile travel during peak traffic flows on the individual motorists who impose them. Consequently, excessive automobile use as contrasted with mass means of transportation is induced, with the result that congestion in downtown areas rises, the private costs of transportation in the core cities increase, and the comparative advantage of central location is reduced.[4]

Similarly, it appears that the incremental costs of serving dispersed residents with utilities are not met by them. This is a consequence of charges for these services which often neglect any individual differences in the cost of service and frequently involve heavy losses in serving outlying areas.[5]

Not only are the costs of constructing utility lines, including water lines and sewers, high per unit in outlying areas, but certain other costs are neglected. The metropolitan area of Chicago, for example, has hundreds of sewage treatment plants, most of them small, inefficiently operated, and discharging into open drains. Compact development not only permits the realization

[4] According to the Regional Plan Association, a commuting motorist driving twenty miles each way to and from work is subsidized up to $1,000 per year.
[5] Mason Gaffney has used a graphic analogy. "The true relative cost of service may best be grasped by envisioning each house connected direct to the water plant with its own separate one-inch pipe—one inch and separate *all the way*." He goes on to comment, "The interior capacity is generally carried by the interior lands and supplied free to the outlanders who simply hook onto the end." In reference 1 at p. 128.

of scale economies in certain public services but frequently increases their quality as, for example, in sewage treatment. These extra costs are, however, seldom if ever levied in a way which would actually affect individual location decisions. Furthermore, dispersed development and dependence on the automobile is, as we have seen in Chapter III, a major contributor to air pollution.

Another defect of dispersed development is that it complicates the provision and enjoyment of genuinely rural experiences. In many areas the sheer length of highway which must be traversed in order to reach truly rural landscapes is forbidding, and the plots of undeveloped land which suburbanization haphazardly leaves scattered about are hardly a good substitute. Certainly, one of the effects of dispersed development is that agricultural use of land mingled with areas of urban development can easily become unprofitable. This withdrawn land—to use Marion Clawson's term for land made unprofitable by urban development—is left unused and often unlovely, frequently accumulating some of the flotsam and jetsam of households and industries, and imposing its external diseconomy on every passer-by. Others have graphically referred to these patches of land as "weedbelts."

The point of this discussion is not so much to insist that urban development has gone awry as it is to raise the possibility that the course of development has not in fact reflected private and public costs fully at points of decision and that as a consequence urban environmental quality and the cost of its management have been adversely affected. Systematic study of improved land and benefits taxation, and especially of user charges as a means of incorporating these external costs into private decisions, is of high importance.

URBAN DEVELOPMENT
AND AESTHETIC PREFERENCES

A problem of the core cities, and one which is particularly difficult to treat systematically, is how to determine what kinds of urban development meet the aesthetic preferences of urban residents. Few would deny that many of our cities are monuments to ugliness and that this condition imposes significant external diseconomies. It is certainly true that urban renewal efforts have been motivated to a considerable degree by a desire to relieve the ugliness of a slum environment.

These projects often result in acres of large residential buildings which carefully segregate commerce from residential uses and which house huge blocks of people of similar cultural and economic levels. Where this occurs there is some evidence that the new areas impose their own varieties of external diseconomies on their residents. Jane Jacobs has argued strongly that diverse city neighborhoods containing different primary uses and having an active semi-public sidewalk life, provide not only situations of interest and pleasure to their residents but in fact are important to their safety. Perhaps we have failed to perceive the utilities which urban environments actually offer low-income people. Some supporting evidence for this position may be drawn from the fact that many housing projects which were initially only uninteresting have become dangerous and ugly. Mrs. Jacobs comments on the possible salvage of such projects as follows: "The general aim should be to bring in uses different from residence, because lack of enough mixed uses is precisely one of the causes of deadness, danger and plain inconvenience. These different uses can occupy entire new street-side buildings, or merely the first floors or basements of buildings. Almost any kind of work use would be especially valuable; also evening uses and general commerce, particularly if these will draw good cross-use from outside the project's former boundaries."[6]

Studies in environmental perception and social psychology would permit us better to gauge the actual values which different configurations of the urban environment can yield. They would be useful to help guide the planning of low-income housing projects and urban renewal, of course. But they could also give us a better conception of what individuals perceive as beauty in a city and how this "trades off" against such other values as con-

---

[6] Jacobs (reference 4), p. 395.

venience and diversity—if these in fact stand in a substitution relationship with respect to each other.

In addition to the external diseconomies thought to be associated with the ugliness of slums, other external benefits in terms of health, safety, and welfare are frequently cited as resulting from urban renewal. It would appear that much more could be done to quantify benefits of this character than has been accomplished to permit society or society's political representatives to form more rational social judgments concerning desirable slum clearance and urban renewal projects.[7]

The magnitude of the slum problem clearly indicates the necessity for intelligent strategy and efficiency in the redevelopment of slum areas. Whether current developments meet these criteria has been questioned by Wilbur R. Thompson as follows:

> Typically we purchase the highest density slum properties simply because they are usually the worst offenders in matters of health, welfare and aesthetics. But the densest slums are also usually the ones which generate the highest rents and (via capitalization of net earnings) the highest property values per acre. We pay dearly to raze those areas. Not only do our current urban renewal budgets shrink distressingly in real purchasing power but, by having to evict large numbers of people we force mass migrations into nearby neighborhoods. Thus we overcrowd the contiguous residential ring, precipitate its early deterioration, and commit future funds to the purchase of similarly over-priced slum properties in the next round. We set up one round after another of expensive condemnations by shoving ahead with brute force, compressing evicted populations ahead of us as we go—a kind of human bulldozing . . . .
>
> Students of housing have long appreciated that if, instead, we were to unload population from these slum areas first and then purchase the properties when they are partly vacant, we would be able to buy slum acreage at much reduced figures. Perhaps we should approach slum clearance from a housing

---

[7] For a review of the studies which have been done on the effects of housing on health and performance, see Wilner and Walkley in reference 2 at pp. 215 ff.

supply vantage point first, and then after we have lowered slum housing densities appreciably we may find the goal of "city beautiful" to be within the límits of our purse. Our current approach may, too much, reflect revulsion against the way slums look—an ugly blot on the landscape that offends the aesthetic senses. A more roundabout but much more efficient, economical, and humane strategy would begin by building new low-income housing on peripheral vacant[8] land, but still close to core-oriented mass transportation. . . . We could still put the highest priority on the rehousing of the inhabitants of any particular slum area by offering space in the new low-rent buildings first to the current residents of the worst slum areas.[9]

Thompson also offers the thought that efficient renewal should perhaps not proceed in solid phalanx but leave carefully planned, small interstices of unrenewed areas which would be uplifted by the surrounding new developments. His rationale is to create leverage by activating private renewal and thereby stretch the scarce public renewal money. He also suggests that the slum families so surrounded would feel the uplifting effect of the immigration of better educated households, especially children in the formative early school years.

Another problem bearing upon urban beauty and urban amenity is the tendency for property devoted to public uses to be undervalued when certain decisions are made. A classic case is the cheap future expressway easement that many transportation planners see in public parks. There is reason to believe that urban residents have a substantial willingness to pay for the creation and maintenance of such park areas and suffer substantial diseconomies when they are destroyed. Moreover it appears that some reasonable measurements of this willingness to pay can be made since it is largely capitalized into the values of contiguous and nearby land.[10]

[8] We would add "or lower density use" here.
[9] Thompson (reference 5), pp. 296–97.
[10] Jack L. Knetsch, "Land Values and Parks in Urban Fringe Areas," *Journal of Farm Economics*, December 1962.

GOVERNMENTAL ORGANIZATION
AND THE COST OF IMPROVEMENT

One of the hypotheses of the present section is that the failure of investment and location decisions to take full account of transportation and utility costs has encouraged dispersed development. But dispersed development may itself have raised the cost of improvement by making it more difficult to organize for the making of such improvements. Urban sprawl in the presence of fixed municipal boundaries has led to growing political fragmentation.

There have been two main responses by students of the problem. One group has strongly favored metropolitan government, characterizing the existing metropolitan regions as legal non-entities. They contend that the people of the metropolis share an important range of problems which go unsolved or are dealt with inefficiently because they have no instrumentality for dealing directly with them. The multiplicity of federal and state governmental agencies, counties, cities, and special districts that govern within metropolitan regions can in this view only lead to partial approaches at best and chaos at worst.

The other group has argued, however, that such units of local government do in fact take each other into account by entering into various contractual and co-operative undertakings or by having recourse to central mechanisms to resolve conflicts. This view holds that the various political jurisdictions in the metropolitan area may function in a coherent manner with consistent and predictable patterns of interacting behavior. To the extent that this is so they may be said to function as a system. It is argued that these elements of the interaction of local governments have been largely neglected and the efficiency of present organization in dealing with metropolitan problems much underrated.[11]

An intermediate position has also been expressed. This places emphasis upon creation of functional authorities (roads, water, sewage, etc.) which may or may not be metropolitan-wide in

[11] Vincent Ostrom, Charles M. Tiebout, and Robert Warren, "The Organization of Government in Metropolitan Areas: A Theoretical Inquiry," *American Political Science Review*, December 1961.

scope depending upon the scope required to internalize the external effects associated with the particular function. In this view the interdependencies between authorities would be dealt with through the indirect means (bargaining, payments, contractual services) implied in the above paragraph.[12]

A complex of important issues is raised by these positions. What constitutes an optimum set of institutions for the governing and management of the urban environment? Is the quality of the urban environment substantially affected by the particular governmental institutions? To what extent will different institutional arrangements tend to communicate with fidelity the demands of urban residents for the public or semi-public services which can be yielded by the environment?

For example, it has been suggested that "clustering" could improve the satisfaction-yielding quality of the suburban environment, at least for a significant number of people. Clustering is done by taking the number of dwelling units permitted by the zoned minimum lot size and distributing them on smaller lots so that some larger and more natural expanses of land are open for collective use. One obstacle to this type of development may be the lack of suitable property institutions. Along the same line, extended and more effective use of zoning may be inhibited by lack of institutional arrangements for equitably redistributing the arbitrary gains and losses associated with zoning and alterations in zones. Losses of potential property value may be especially large when land is zoned for agricultural, forest, or open space use or when zoning is used to save buildings of historical or architectural interest.

Finally, there is the problem of integrating the operation of particular institutions within the context of larger systems, such as those concerned with the quality of water within watershed or river basin areas, the quality of the air in regional air sheds, and the quality of the regional landscape environment.

The simple fact is that we know very little about designing institutions. Political science and economics face some of their greatest challenges in this area.

[12] Vernon (reference 6), pp. 52 ff.

Some Selected References on the Physical Environment of Urban Places

1. *Approaches to the Study of Urbanization.* The Center for Government Research. University of Kansas, 1964.
2. Duhl, Leonard J., (editor). *The Urban Condition.* New York: Basic Books, Inc., 1963.
3. *Guiding Metropolitan Growth.* New York: Committee for Economic Development, 1960.
4. Jacobs, Jane. *The Death and Life of Great American Cities.* New York: Vintage Books, 1963.
5. Thompson, Wilbur R. *A Preface to Urban Economics.* Baltimore: The Johns Hopkins Press for Resources for the Future, Inc., 1965.
6. Vernon, Raymond. *The Myth and Reality of Our Urban Problems.* Cambridge: Harvard–MIT Joint Center for Urban Studies, 1962.
7. Wingo, Lowdon, Jr. (editor). *Cities and Space.* Baltimore: The Johns Hopkins Press for Resources for the Future, Inc., 1963.

CHAPTER VI

SOME PROBLEMS
ASSOCIATED WITH
THE USE OF RURAL AREAS

Of the many problems in rural areas to which the framework of external effects can be applied profitably, we touch briefly on a few where decisions have long-run consequences that are difficult to reverse. These include certain aspects of highway construction, mining activity, wildlife, reservoirs, and wilderness lands. The difficulties in studying these areas are challenging, for the number of individuals or households subjected to external effects is uncertain, as is the precise nature of the effects themselves.

It is evident from the title of this chapter that it is on a different footing from the other chapters of this study. There is something of the nature of a grab bag about this group of problems, for "use of the rural environment" has no unifying element—apart from the general framework of external effects—similar to that possessed by each of the problem areas that has been discussed so far. In the cases of water and air pollution, there is a carrying medium for the pollutants which gives a useful unity to the wide variety of sub-problems that are to be found within each category. In some respects the unity is deceptive, for air pollution problems differ considerably from city to city, and the same is true of water pollution problems in different localities. Still, the fact of a common carrier—water in the one case and air in the other—provides ample justification for speaking of a water pollution problem and an air pollution problem. The main reason for this is that the fact of a common carrier for the pollutants requires a certain unity of administration in dealing with the problems.

In the case of pesticides, the apparent unity of the problem grows out of the fact of a pesticide industry and out of a general pest problem which comes to a number of separate foci in the practices followed by farmers and others in their efforts to deal with the various types of pests.

With the problems that were discussed in connection with the city, a focus is provided by the fact of localization. The compactness of the city insures that there will be many interconnections between the different facets of the urban problem that involve important external effects, and in any case a considerable unity is bound to be imposed on the group of problems if only because there is an identifiable group of people who live in and use the facilities provided by the city.

It is possible to look on rural areas in this way, too. After all, there is an identifiable group of people who live in rural areas, and a much larger and growing group of people who are making increasing use of rural areas as places through which they travel or whose facilities they use in various special locations.[1]

As our population grows, these facilities of the rural areas are going to be used more and more intensively. It has seemed to us, however, that it is not particularly useful to discuss in a general way the problems associated with this use. Principally because procedures for dealing with the various problems or rural areas are not and probably will not be organized on a general basis, we have concluded that it is more useful to discuss the separate problems enumerated above, each of which possesses a considerable unity which is reflected in the instrumentalities and in the methods that are used or might be used to deal with them.

[1] Philip M. Hoff, Governor of Vermont, has observed that the state of Vermont seems to be turning into a weekend haven for New Yorkers and other big city residents of the northeast. It is becoming more and more difficult to find a house in Vermont that needs a coat of paint. See *Washington Post*, March 16, 1965, p. A4.

HIGHWAYS

The user of highways may be subjected to congestion costs imposed by users on each other and to a barrage of monotonous and unattractive scenes associated with the highway itself and with nearby construction. Effects like these vary enormously in importance from place to place, but for a number of reasons it seems likely that their incidence will grow as time goes on. The yearly mileage of every passenger car increased very little from 1940 to 1962 on the average, but the total number of passenger car miles increased to where the 1962 total was 2½ times that of 1940 and on urban roads was about 2⅓ times that of 1940. At the same time, miles of urban and rural road increased much less, with the result that vehicle mileage per mile of road has increased substantially.[2] The increase in total passenger car mileage is, therefore, the result of more cars on the roads, which in turn reflects a rapidly growing population and rapidly rising levels of income. Rising incomes have facilitated multiple automobile ownership by some households.

The increasing density of traffic brings with it an elaborate set of external diseconomies. Apart from the external costs imposed by drivers on each other, an increasing volume of traffic generates a larger number of structures intended to service this traffic—filling stations, motels, grocery stores, beer parlors, miniature golf courses, and so on. In many cases this results in subjecting the automobile travelers to a steady stream of impressions which for many are depressing. Unless institutional control is exercised at state or federal levels excessive numbers of exits and entrances to highways tend to be created by local interests. These contribute to congestion, accidents, and unattractive appearance.

The multiplication of facilities to service the growing stream of traffic also results in many more signs and lights. These are an eyesore. They are also a danger on the highways, for brilliant multicolored lights confuse and distract attention from traffic signals. It is even doubtful whether a multiplicity of signs is

[2] U.S. Department of Commerce, *Statistical Abstract of the United States* (Washington: U.S. Government Printing Office, 1964), pp. 556 and 563.

economically effective, since the efforts of the advertisers largely cancel each other out. The information the signs offer presumably could be as well provided in other ways less aesthetically offensive.

While these problems are most serious near centers of population, even in rural areas unattractive signs and business establishments, though lower in density, may have a particularly deleterious effect because they often are imposed upon a beautiful stretch of countryside. The bogus "Dangerous Desert Ahead" and "Indian Trading Post" signs seen for miles on either side of the larger cities along Route 66 through the Southwest are especially offensive examples of an all-too-common violation of the traveler's sensibilities.

Apart from signs and structures alongside highways, there are many cases where the design and placement of the highway itself can ruin or preserve a beautiful countryside. There is often a choice open. A highway can be unobtrusive and also be the means for revealing the beauty of a landscape to many who might not otherwise see it. But if highway designers consider that the preservation of natural beauty is never worth even a small sacrifice in speed or money, one stretch of road will be pretty much like any other—monotonous black or white ribbons flowing between equally monotonous ribbons of green grass.

Some people profess to be indifferent to what they see when on a highway. However large this group may be, there is another group that is not indifferent. Unfortunately, there really is no way by which the preferences of this latter group can be given effective expression in the market. The political institutions controlling highway construction through rural areas often do not take account of these preferences, in part because the external diseconomies are to a major extent imposed upon residents of other political jurisdictions. Still, it is possible to study the nature and strength of these preferences, granted that they are not so easily quantified as the demand for, say, wheat. And there may be much to be learned from comparative studies of why some jurisdictions handle the problems of highway design and environmental quality better than others.

MINING

Both in areas surrounding urban centers and in more remote regions, mining sometimes seriously disfigures the landscape. For example, sand and gravel pits and clay pits are usually found near their large markets, as are limestone quarries for the manufacture of cement. Sometimes these "ubiquitous" mining activities, especially sand and gravel, are quite close to residential areas and produce serious external effects involving the sightliness of the area and the noise of operations and of passing trucks. They are also a substantial safety problem, for young children are often attracted to such workings.

Where mining activities are close to populated areas they are usually regulated to some degree, but the volume of householders' protests that normally accompanies the opening of new workings near residential areas suggests that regulation does not succeed in eliminating the external effects nor in adequately compensating those who are injured. This does not mean necessarily that the regulation is causing the minerals to be produced in the wrong places or in the wrong quantities (viewing the members of society as a group), but even so, the redistributions of income that are involved in opening sand and gravel pits or any other form of mining near an established residential area are certainly arbitrary.

Intensive study of the results of regulation in some selected areas might reveal ways by which a better accommodation of the various interests could be reached. Among the possibilities to be assessed are (1) the effect of disseminating information on the location of potential deposits and (2) an attempt to give some indication of the sequence (not necessarily with dates) in which zoning changes are likely to be made as the development of an area proceeds.

Coal mining differs from the ubiquitous mining activities in that it is often conducted at sites relatively remote from its markets. In the absence of regulation, the decline of a coal mining operation or community tends to leave a legacy of ugliness. This is perhaps most obvious in the case of strip mining operations which churn up the landscape, dig gaping holes, pollute streams, and leave the countryside in a mutilated condition for many years if remedial measures are not taken.

Many states are beginning to regulate strip mining more closely than has been the case in the past, and are requiring measures to restore to some degree the appearance of the landscape after a strip mining operation is completed. The task of introducing such regulation is made easier by the experience of a number of strip mining companies who have found that restoration can in some cases be profitable to the mining company itself.

While control of strip mining practices—both imposed control and self control—has reduced significantly some of the external costs imposed on others, there has been little attempt to evaluate such control in terms of economic efficiency. This is partly because regulation is comparatively recent. But experience and data are growing and may have reached a point where useful studies of the costs and benefits associated with various patterns of regulation can be made. The diversity of strip mining operations—especially in location and the nature and extent of external effects generated—complicates the regulatory problem. The goal of regulation, operating in conjunction with private incentive, should be to maximize the contribution of the strip area to national product, taking into account mining methods, undesirable side effects imposed, and the stream of product after restoration, if any. This goal may require different treatment for different properties recognizing that regulation should be restricted to securing a desirable handling of external effects on others. Regulation should not interfere with aspects of the mining operation or of restoration which do not produce external effects.

The effects of hard-rock mining operations on the appearance of a landscape can be just as adverse as those of mining coal or the ubiquitous minerals such as sand and gravel, clay, and limestone. There is an important difference, however: hard-rock mining usually takes place in remote areas where there are few people to regret the loss of natural beauty.

We cannot expect to enjoy our present level of material goods production without creating mines and, in the process, large amounts of waste materials which remain after extracting the desired materials from the ore. But we can and should ask that mining activities in remote areas refrain from the spoliation of places of natural grandeur. It is incongruous, for example, that a uranium mine should be operating on the rim of the Grand Canyon, an area visited by thousands of people each year. While it is true that the most beautiful of the country's western areas remain largely undisturbed by existing mining activities—they are too remote—many of them are unprotected against the possibility of future mining exploitation, even those officially designated as "wilderness areas."

As it becomes feasible to extend mining to greater distances from present consumption and transportation centers, areas of great natural beauty may be threatened with disfigurement more frequently than in the past—often by mines whose real contribution to the product of the country will be almost negligible. In deciding whether the beauty of the area is worth preserving, we must be careful to value correctly the contribution of the mineral deposit to the nation's product. This contribution is not measured by the market value of the ore produced, nor by the wages that are paid. The proper measure of what we sacrifice (as a group) by not mining the deposit is the profit or rent left over after deducting all expenses (including the competitive return on capital) from revenues. This profit or rent is frequently small even for mines with a large output. In other words, equivalent materials usually could be extracted elsewhere at very little additional cost.

WILDLIFE

Many people derive keen pleasure from the observation of wildlife and from hunting and fishing. It is a pleasure that in some cases can be purchased. For example, some private hunting and fishing preserves are run as clubs or cater to the general public. Where wildlife does not require an extensive range or where private preserves are so located as to be able to make use of public range, the game can in effect be "produced." But for many kinds of birds and mammals "production" of a supply involves external factors that are beyond the control of a single enterprise. Individual entrepreneurs will have little incentive to produce game which may benefit not them but others. Wildlife thus has a "fugitive" or public character about it, as every hunter knows. The supply of many birds and mammals is consequently the unintended result of the whole complex of nature and human activity, little or none of which, in the absence of government intervention, would be specifically directed toward maintaining or providing favorable conditions for the production of wildlife.

All of us know how great has been the depredation caused by man among some varieties of wildlife. In the United States the numbers of buffalo, whooping crane, grizzly, and mountain lion have all been reduced. The wild duck population is considerably lower than it was before many of the nesting grounds were drained. Predators have been eliminated over large areas of the country in which they were once plentiful, as a result of extermination activities and changes in habitat. It is notable that activity tending to eliminate or reduce predators has seldom if ever been carried out with any clear understanding of even the most direct effects on the other organisms of the area. Mountain lions are found now in only a few areas. Wolves are almost completely absent from the continental United States, and even coyotes have been tremendously reduced in numbers, mainly through poisoning. Prairie dogs continue to survive in only a few places. Fur-bearing animals such as beaver, mink, and otter are no longer to be found in many locations in which they were once plentiful. Only those creatures which have shown the ability to adapt to the changes in environment brought about by human activity survive in large numbers. Rabbits continue to do well. The white-tailed deer abounds in many sections, and it is thought that there are more of them in some states than before white men came, for the activities of man generally seem to increase the supply of food for deer.

It is not clear whether our environment will be able to supply numbers of animals and birds sufficient to meet the demands of hunters, fishermen, and observers. One major problem is to evaluate the willingness of individuals to pay the opportunity cost of increasing numbers of wildlife. A second major problem is the conception and formation of institutional arrangements which can bring about increases in the supply of wildlife in response to demand. It may be desirable, for example, to collect fees from beneficiaries to a much larger extent than is now done and to pay compensation to farmers who provide food for game but have little or no opportunity to profit from it. There is a need for studies of wildlife production economics as well as of the demand for wildlife.

FLOWING STREAMS AND RESERVOIRS

A glance at a map showing the numerous large reservoirs in the West reveals that many of our streams have been converted to slack water over long stretches. This is true or will be true for most of the Columbia River, most of the Snake River and some of its tributaries, and for most of the Colorado and some of its tributaries. The same thing is happening in the Ozarks. The eastern part of the country has not yet been affected to a similar extent although in some instances where navigation is important, particularly on the Ohio, long stretches of slack water have already been created. In the years to come there will be strong pressures for the construction of extensive systems of dams to make the seasonal flows of our eastern rivers more regular. Elaborate plans have already been drawn up for the Delaware and the Potomac basins.

There is danger that the aesthetic and recreational values associated with flowing streams, which necessarily are sacrificed when a dam is built, will not receive proper attention in the complicated process of deciding whether or not to build a dam. With a few notable exceptions such considerations seem to have carried almost no weight in the decisions to construct Western dams. It remains to be seen whether aesthetic considerations will effectively influence the decisions on the many proposals for dam construction which will be considered in the East in the years to come. It is encouraging that current federal government procedures for calculating costs and benefits provide, in principle, for the consideration of aesthetic and recreational values sacrificed or gained. Different types of recreational values may sometimes be gained from a reservoir and in a few cases even aesthetic values, but experience to date shows rather clearly that recreational and aesthetic values sacrificed by dam construction have rarely been taken into account.

If there were a way by which those who desire the preservation of a Glen Canyon, an Echo Park, or a Potomac Valley could make their demands effective by an act of purchase, there would be no problem. Since this does not appear to be possible, it is necessary to rely on the political process, including procedures within the Executive branch of the federal government, for decisions on dam construction. We suspect that the decisions that are being reached can be improved upon and that improvement can be hastened by work done by economists outside the government in evaluating proposals for construction.

One danger is that decisions will be made case by case, ignoring in each instance what apparently are unimportant aesthetic considerations. If this happens, we could find ourselves after a few decades confronted with a landscape utterly and unfavorably altered from its former state—the result of a complex of projects whose effects are virtually irreversible.

"NATURAL" AREAS

The problems of natural areas, including wilderness, and seashores share certain similarities, chief among which is the fact that in each case private enterprise may not be best suited to meet the wide variety of demands for the services these areas can provide.

Some of the demands for the services of natural areas can be quite well satisfied by private enterprise, however. Private campgrounds, fishing camps, hunting camps, and resorts have been with us for a long time, and so have private beaches. In addition, many of the demands for the services of natural areas are satisfied by state governments and the federal government through the provision of campgrounds, state parks, and similar areas. The costs of providing these services, incidentally, are covered to a considerable extent by fees levied upon the users even though the management of the property is in the hands of a governmental unit. Another step in this direction was made early in 1965, with the federal government's sale of $7 automobile stickers, entitling purchasers to enter any federal recreation area during the period of a year. The funds raised by this means will contribute to a Land and Water Conservation Fund set up to preserve and acquire land for recreational use.

Beyond the comparatively simple popular demands on natural areas, such as providing a campground or a spot by a stream or lake for a picnic, there is another which presents a different and more difficult problem. This is the demand for large and, to varying degrees, uncrowded pieces of country where a person can "stretch his spirit." In this country, unlike some others, the real or implied "No Trespassing" signs that surround every piece of private property constitute a very real barrier to the wanderer who desires the freedom to walk over and to feel that he is a part of a larger area that extends beyond where he happens to be at the moment. Yet there are some who would be willing to pay substantial sums of money for the privilege of walking over lands that give the impression of being limitless.

Is it possible for the private market to satisfy these demands? Judging by experience in the eastern part of the United States, it is not. In the West the problem has not yet arisen because there are still large tracts in the hands of the federal government to which people with this particular taste can go. If their quality of sheer size should be destroyed—perhaps by the intrusion of highways or other accouterments of civilization—it is not likely that private enterprise would be able to assemble comparably large areas to which nature lovers would have access.

The problem of preserving large wild areas for the enjoyment of the few who demand and use them is a difficult one. It is true that only a small percentage of the population uses such areas in any one year. This use may be, however, a once or a few in a lifetime experience for many people. They may be willing to pay an annual fee for the preservation of these opportunities even if they see them and directly experience them infrequently or perhaps not at all. There is nothing strange about this, for many solicitations for funds use the mails and use them successfully even though the donors of the funds never see directly the things for which the funds are spent. Wild areas are not necessarily in a different category. The destruction of wilderness imposes an external diseconomy on such people whether they ever see the area or not. But it is very difficult to discover how extensive is this demand without the active participation of such individuals in a market.

It is true that, compared with other highly developed countries, the United States has a tremendous total acreage in wild land. On the other hand, if one looks at those areas that were designated as "wilderness tracts" in 1960 by the Outdoor Recreation Resources Review Commission, it is obvious that few are in tracts that could be regarded as large by most standards. Table 3 shows this rather clearly. The first column lists class intervals in terms of acreage; no area of less than 100,000 acres is included. The second column converts each area into an equivalent square. Thus, the first class interval is made up of those wilderness areas with a total number of acres of 100,000 up to 200,000. An area of 100,000 acres is equal to that of a square with a side of 12.5 miles, a square that would be rather confining to that minority of the population which enjoys extensive hiking.

The areas presently classified as "wilderness" often are of outstanding natural beauty and attractiveness. There is, accordingly, a persistent pressure to develop access to them. Obviously, it is impossible to satisfy this demand for very long—essentially a de-

TABLE 3. FREQUENCY OF WILDERNESS AREAS BY SIZE

Thousands of acres	Approximate equivalent square (miles on a side)	Frequency
100—	12	23
200—	18	15
300—	22	7
400—	25	6
500—	28	2
700—	33	5
1,000—	40	1
1,500—	48	4
2,000—	56	1
2,500—	62	0
		64

Source: Tabulated from ORRRC Study Report 3, p. 43. (See reference 7, p. 80.)

mand to have the comforts of civilization away from crowds and yet to be on the edge of or in a wild area—for as demand is satisfied, the remaining wild area is steadily reduced. In the United States, "development" and the provision of access have seemed to be almost inexorable up to this point. It seems inevitable, therefore, that the problem of preserving wilderness areas and areas of natural beauty will become more acute as time goes on.

A problem analogous to that of wilderness is presented by shorelines. Less than 2 per cent of the total ocean shorelines of the contiguous states is in public ownership for recreation. It is true that access is possible on a considerable part of the privately owned shorelines and that there is a well-developed market for beach activities; but there is a component of demand for undeveloped shoreline similar to that for wilderness, and this is not at all likely to be satisfied by the offerings of private enterprise.

The demand for wilderness areas and for long, untouched shorelines is a demand to be free from the external diseconomies of development. If these demands are to be satisfied under public auspices, an estimate of their strength must be made to set against the sacrifice of revenues the areas could earn if they were used in other ways. If in some manner it was discovered that the devotees of wild areas and untouched shoreline were willing to pay a sum of money at least this large, total real national product would be increased by leaving the areas wild and untouched. But even if ways could be found to organize the payment of such a sum, the further question would arise as to whether the payment should, in fact, be exacted.

It is important to note that there may be not only one but two relevant tests of what a natural area is worth to these people. On the one hand, the question can be posed as it has been above: How much money would these people *be willing to pay* in order to secure the services of this type of area? On the other hand, the question could be asked in this way: How much would these people *have to be paid,* in the event the services of the area were taken from them, in order to make them feel that they were as well off as they were before its loss? If, in such circumstances, the services of the area constituted a large part of their real income, it is quite likely that the amount of money these people would have to be paid would be larger than the sum they would be willing to pay in order to secure the services of the area.

To take an extreme case, consider a person who has only a subsistence income, but who is able to enjoy the services of a wilderness area or a park. If payment for the services were required of such a person, he could pay very little if anything. If, on the other hand, he were to be deprived of the services of the area and be compensated fully—i.e., to the extent that he would regard himself as well off as he was before—the compensation required might well be larger than his actual money income.

The second compensation test frequently seems relevant in condemnation proceedings. When people are ousted from places to which they have become deeply attached, any money compensation that may be made is never commensurate with the distress caused them by the forced move. In such cases an external cost is imposed on these people and real income is simply destroyed.

It is important to realize that these valuation problems may be present with many kinds of external benefits, whether they come from wilderness areas, city parks, birdlife, beaches, national parks, or beautiful urban environments. To some people the

psychic satisfaction they derive from these areas forms a significant part of their real incomes. If we hope to move toward
optimum environmental quality it is necessary to learn much more
about these problems. Needless to say, it would be extremely
difficult to obtain honest estimates of the amount of damages involved in our second compensation test. Accordingly, compensation in condemnation proceedings tends to hew pretty much to
market value.

As we look over the varied kinds of demands and external
effects that have been discussed in connection with the rural environment, one feature stands out as common to all of them:
They all involve preferences which are far from uniform among
the population, far less than are those for good health, for example. In this respect they are similar to certain aspects of the
demand for urban environmental quality.

In thinking about the severity of these problems, about the
direction in which they are likely to develop, and about the
means we might use to deal with them, it is essential to bear in
mind that a wide spectrum of demands is involved. The demand
for natural areas runs the gamut from wilderness areas and
national parks to spots for picnics or places where one can walk
for a few minutes in the evening. The goal of private and public
action should be to satisfy all of these demands so as to get the
largest excess of benefit over costs. This goal cannot be achieved
or even approached if only that type of service is provided which
is demanded by most of the customers. This makes no more
sense—and as bad sense—as supplying houses in one design re-
gardless of variations in taste. Unfortunately, there seems to be
a tendency for governmental agencies to cater to the most numerous group in their particular constituency and to neglect the
demands of others. This tendency needs to be resisted, as indeed
it is by good administrators.

Some Selected References on Problems of Rural Areas

1. Blake, Peter. *God's Own Junkyard: The Planned Deterioration of America's Landscape.* New York: Holt, Rinehart, and Winston, 1964.

2. Council of State Governments. *Surface Mining—Extent and Economic Importance, Impact on Natural Resources, and Proposals for Reclamation of Mined Lands.* Proceedings of a Conference on Surface Mining, April 13–14, 1964. Chicago, 1964.

3. Fox, Irving K. and Herfindahl, Orris C. "Attainment of Efficiency in Satisfying Demands for Water Resources," *American Economic Review*, May 1964.

4. Fund, David T. *A Revised Bibliography of Strip-Mine Reclamation.* Central States Forest Experiment Station, Misc. Release No. 35. Columbus, Ohio, 1962.

5. Lucas, Robert C. "Wilderness Perception and Use: The Example of the Boundary Waters Canoe Area," *Natural Resources Journal*, January 1964.

6. Meiners, Robert G. "Strip Mining Legislation," *Natural Resources Journal*, January 1964.

7. Outdoor Recreation Resources Review Commission, *Outdoor Recreation for America* (Report of the Commission); *Wilderness and Recreation—A Report on Resources, Values, and Problems* (ORRRC Study Report 3); *Sport Fishing—Today and Tomorrow* (ORRRC Study Report 7); *Hunting in the United States—Its Present and Future Role* (ORRRC Study Report 6). Washington: U.S. Government Printing Office, 1962.

8. Stratton, Owen and Sirotkin, Phillip. *The Echo Park Controversy.* The Inter-University Case Program. University, Alabama: University of Alabama Press, 1959.

CHAPTER VII

A RESEARCH STRATEGY

The results of the applied research that has been done on the problems discussed in the preceding chapters have emphasized only certain aspects of the problems; consequently the gaps in understanding are great and the links between foci frail at best. In these circumstances, some suggestions as to the directions of research may be beneficial. Not that we can specify precisely where the best research opportunities may lie—this would presume a degree of understanding disproportionate to the complexities of the problems—but we do, in formulating our research strategy, point out some possible approaches.

Perhaps the main advantage in trying to formulate a research strategy is to prevent the continued neglect of certain aspects of environment problems. Substantial lacunae in research efforts are especially likely in these problems because they require the simultaneous application of principles and relationships from natural science, engineering, and the social sciences. The investigator needs at least a limited knowledge of disciplines other than his own. To gain this is a demanding undertaking. One major reason why the social sciences, and especially economics, have had so little impact on policy making in these areas may well be that comparatively few social scientists have troubled to learn the natural science and engineering subject matter in a reasonable degree of depth.

The formulation of a research strategy is complicated by the fact that direct interdependencies exist among the various fields we have discussed as well as within them. For example, the specific placement of an industrial area may affect both air and water pollution in ways that should be considered when making location decisions. Incineration of sewage sludge or other waste products may protect water courses but pollute the air. Air pollution control in urban areas will certainly change the nature and location of industrial waste discharge to water courses. Compact land use in urban areas may contribute some direct aesthetic satisfactions and simultaneously reduce certain pollution problems such as those associated with cesspools and sediment.

The list of such interdependencies could be greatly extended; nevertheless, we believe that at this stage in our knowledge the areas of water and air pollution, pesticide use, and rural and urban environmental quality are useful divisions for research because the fundamental concepts and research methodologies one can apply are sufficiently similar.

It is when one addresses the question of appropriate institutional arrangements that the problem of interdependencies among the fields unavoidably emerges. Even so, it seems probable that a broader synthesis should only be attempted when conceptualization of the problem and analysis of the revelant systems and their components have developed to a point where the institutional question can be engaged on a sound basis. In the meantime, our research strategy may be applied to each field individually so long as obvious opportunities to gain understanding of relations among them are not overlooked.

ELEMENTS OF THE RESEARCH STRATEGY

To enumerate the elements of a research strategy may seem to be superfluous since the elements themselves are obvious enough. But since the researcher's understanding is inevitably affected by his specialization, there is some justification for formalizing the obvious: we can thereby raise questions about the adequacy of current understandings.

The following elements are involved:

1. Conceptualization of the subject-matter field by specifying the variables and relationships that would be involved in arriving at decisions on possible changes in the management of the

particular problem area. This process may be called, in the jargon of the day, building a "normative decision model." When available empirical information is confronted with such a model, research needs can be identified and evaluated more easily.

2. Study of relationships and parameters specified in the decision model. There are important gaps in natural science and engineering as well as social science knowledge.

3. Application of the model and empirical information generated to one or more actual case study situations. Not only may these studies provide valuable knowledge for particular cases, but they may help to identify further problems overlooked at the more abstract stage and to bring tools and techniques to an operational stage.

4. The final stage is study of institutional design. What should be the scope of powers of implementing agencies? How can they be designed to work toward results which may be deemed in the public interest rather than narrow special interest?

Each of these elements is discussed in more detail below. Illustrative material is drawn from preceding chapters and from the research program of Resources for the Future—especially its studies of water pollution in which some progress has been made through the sequence outlined above. At the end of the chapter, we shall discuss briefly an appropriate division of labor in research on these problems.

CONCEPTUALIZATION AND INITIAL MARSHALLING OF DATA

An effective program of research dealing with the important problems of environmental quality must be firmly embedded in a conceptual framework which specifies the research goals and provides a means of factoring out "researchable" pieces contributing to the achievement of the objective. The framework sketched in this study is based, in general, upon the view that resources are to be used with a full knowledge of all the costs such use imposes, whether the costs are internal or external to the activity immediately in question. The fundamental objective, taken from welfare economics, is that satisfaction derived from a resource use activity, as measured by individuals' "willingness to pay," shall be a maximum net of costs. This is the concept embodied in a number of official documents relating to the benefit-cost analysis of water resource projects.

This concept has two significant attributes. First, it is consistent with some fundamental value judgments that most people would accept about our society, including the judgment that individual tastes and values are to govern the use of resources in a free society. Secondly, it is the only theory of social values we know of which is sufficiently detailed, precise, and logical to yield clear decision criteria which could form the basis for public and private action consistent with these values. However, being a theory, it is, of course, a rather radical simplification of reality. It has been said that there is nothing to be accomplished by drawing a map on a one-to-one scale. On the other hand, it would be foolish to use a map as though it were a complete guide to reality. This simply means, in the present context, that users of the theory must extend, adapt, and modify as reality may demand.

It is our view that generally the market produces a reasonable approximation to the ideal: production of the desired set of goods and services by such means that the net willingness to pay is at a maximum. It is important to understand, however, that the application of this concept does not require an actual market for the goods and services being evaluated. Indeed, there are some well-recognized circumstances where market processes yield results far removed from the ideal, one of which is externality, well illustrated in the previous chapters and at the heart of the environmental quality problem. Yet even when there are distorting conditions like externalities, the theory of optimum production can provide guidance for collective action.

The utility of the "framework" or conceptualization stage of the research strategy is that it can provide a reasonably clear and systematic view of how facts and relationships can be brought together in such a way as to lead toward the objective of obtaining maximum value from the resource. The framework must necessarily be inadequate, for it cannot do more than reflect present understanding. Even so, it can organize this understanding, show how it is related to decision needs, and point to important gaps.

The conceptualization stage will also be an appropriate one for judging the adequacy and appropriateness of the various tools of applied mathematics and systems analysis for the problem. Where numerous direct interdependencies (externalities) exist in the same system and where the intensity of the links are dependent upon complex phenomena of a biological, meteorological, or hydrological character, the mathematical and computational problems associated with seeking an optimum can be very challenging and constitute an important area of research in their own right.

Finally, where longer range planning becomes important—for example, if durable capital investments such as dams or transportation systems or changes in land use, or possible cumulative effects on health, are involved—the adequacy of our ability to project economic, demographic, and technological factors as well as our ability to understand and deal with dynamic processes of adjustment comes into question. Since uncertainty will inevitably characterize decisions which must be made in the anticipation of future events, the special problems of uncertainty which may characterize a particular field invite inquiry, as do possible ways of arriving at decisions in spite of them.

The studies by Kneese and Headley on water pollution and pesticides are examples of the type of framework study we have in mind.[1]

DETAILED STUDY OF
RELATIONSHIPS AND PARAMETERS

From a framework study it will be possible to identify some relationships and values which would play an important part in any effort to achieve an optimum but which are not well enough

---

[1] See Selected References, pp. 23 and 52.

understood to actually do so. These gaps invite study and can be illustrated by the framework studies referred to above and from the preceding chapters.

Among the relationships will be a number of a technological, biological, hydrological, and meteorological character. These can be productive topics of research in engineering and natural science. As an example, consider the ability to forecast the changes in water quality throughout entire stream systems as they are affected by changes in waste load at particular points and the various relevant hydrological and meteorological influencing phenomena. This is clearly important to any effort to manage water quality in an optimum fashion and, in fact, has become an important area of research endeavor.

In regard to economics, it is apparent that many items of willingness-to-pay and cost information are unavailable and that obtaining them may be a difficult task, if indeed it is possible at all. It is convenient to discuss these difficulties under the categories of demand and supply.

Demand. Many of the demands for avoidance of pollution of air and water can in principle be measured with considerable accuracy. Damages to industrial users often fall in this category. Indeed, effects on production processes are sometimes the object of day-to-day calculation. Even so, it often will be necessary to determine values for ranges of the quality variable which have not in fact been experienced, and to calculate how the user would optimally adjust to them. Calculation does not characterize the household world to the same extent. Nevertheless, the possibility of reasonably accurate estimation of many of the costs that pollution imposes on households seems good. The question in each case is what a rational consumer or producer would be willing to pay in order to avoid the damage that is done by the pollutant in question. For example, the costs of dealing with corrosion, scaling, soiling, or deterioration of product quality do not pose any particularly unusual problems for estimation. Often overlooked, however, is the fact that some of these effects are variable with respect to time and must be weighted according to their probabilities. Some promising work on this type of demand or "loss" function has begun, especially in the area of water pollution. Here, a series of industry studies has been initiated and studies of willingness-to-pay for improved municipal water supply and for recreation water quality improvement have been undertaken. Much work remains to be done in studies of both water pollution and air pollution.

Certain external effects resulting from quality deterioration due to intense use of natural areas or capital facilities (e.g., highways) do not involve an actual flow of physical bodies to affected parties. Such congestion effects are common in the use of wilderness areas and urban transportation and space. Measurement of the costs imposed on others is much more difficult here than in the case of actual physical damages, but it is by no means hopeless. Some promising efforts have been started, and it should be possible to learn more about the effect of congestion on preferences and the willingness to pay for alternative conditions. Possible psychic and other health effects may yield in some measure to comparative case studies. The same is true of the effects of ugliness, lack of privacy, and personal safety associated with the extreme congestion characteristic of slum conditions.

The study of demand is more difficult for several of the problem areas that have been discussed. The outlook for developing reliable information on the long-term health effects of persistent pollutants and pesticides, including radiation effects, is not good at all. In many of these cases a control group cannot be used, although for some substances it may be possible to establish differences in exposure. The prospect is even more remote for developing reliable information about the effect on body and mental health of the psychic response to the environment. In fact, no very satisfactory means have been devised even for evaluating the benefits of good health, although a number of calculations can be made which are helpful for making certain decisions. However, to pursue such evaluations in regard to the health effects of particular substances does not get us very far so long as we know so little about the effects themselves. The first order of business is to understand those effects better; then economic research on demand and value can make its contribution.

In some cases the problem of gauging demand is made difficult because there is little or no direct activity which leaves an observable track. By way of example, consider what values people might attach to the appearance of the city of Washington or to the preservation of a wilderness area. In such cases individuals who have never directly seen the valued objects may be willing to pay for their improvement or preservation. Since demands of this kind are "public" in character, it is difficult to induce people to reveal their true preferences. Still, we believe that sample surveys possibly could yield useful information on the importance individuals attach to values of this type.

Even in the absence of numerical data bearing on such demands, a vital piece of information for deciding whether or not to meet the demand is the net cost of providing the service in question. For example, in the case of maintaining areas as wilderness this cost is the net value of national product that could have been produced if the area were not used as wilderness. That is, it is the sum of the rent that could have been collected on the land and the maintenance outlays involved in using it as wilderness. Unless the area contains particularly rich and accessible mineral and forest resources, the rent foregone is likely to be small.

In sum, the positive and negative values associated with external effects on environmental quality are ordinarily difficult to gauge and some can never be measured with precision. Nevertheless, there are opportunities for research which should yield information useful for more rational and effective management of environmental quality.

Supply. Usually the supply or cost side of these problems is somewhat easier to study than the demand side, the main reason being that the costs involved are commonly represented by market prices. In cases where businessmen have not already investigated the cost of taking certain actions affecting environmental quality, it is sometimes feasible for research organizations or public agencies to do so. A seriously complicating factor is that the best way to solve the problem may not be available to the individual plant or community but may have to be designed anew on a region-wide basis. An effort to improve water quality may involve consideration of measures to change the hydrology and waste-assimilative capacity of the receiving water (a set of alternatives best implemented by a public agency) as well as treatment and other measures at individual points of waste discharge. There is a great need for studies to develop estimates and empirical information on the best combinations of measures for improving environmental quality and the costs associated with them. Often such studies are best made by focusing on actual cases.

In many instances those economic units that are the origin of external effects have not concerned themselves with the cost of altering them because there is no private gain in doing so. The result is that in many cases we simply do not know what it would cost to reduce the external effect by x per cent. It is remarkable, for example, how little usable knowledge exists concerning the costs industry must incur to reduce waste discharges to air or water by various amounts, or about the cost and effectiveness of unorthodox measures such as certain means for improving the waste-assimilative capacity of streams. DDT provides another example. If the rate at which DDT reaches humans were to be reduced by 50 per cent, what would be the net cost in terms of lowered crop yield, assuming that the money formerly spent on DDT is now spent in the best possible way—perhaps on other insecticides or the purchase of seed of a different variety? So far as we are aware, a useful answer to this seemingly simple but actually very complex question is not now possible.

Information of this kind is essential if a comparison between costs and benefits is to be made. And even if we do not know demand functions in quantitative terms, it still will be useful for policy purposes to know what it would cost to change the supply of a pollutant which might be dangerous or impose a substantial but unmeasured external cost in other ways. Suppose, for example, we know that ingestion of DDT by humans could be reduced to zero at the cost of a 1 per cent increase in the retail food bill. While we do not *know* what this would mean in terms of health, we would know the cost of purchasing this particular kind of insurance. Along similar lines, before licensing a new agricultural or food processing chemical which could possibly involve some danger, an attempt might be made to calculate the cost of delaying introduction for, say, a couple of years while further tests are performed. In cases where such calculable costs are minor a particularly strong burden of proof could be put on the applicant.

If the costs of small changes in regulatory standards can be related to a measurable variable (e.g., a pollutant) which in turn has effects on life and health of unknown magnitude, some important tests of consistency can be performed. We could begin to determine whether the incremental cost of reducing the measurable variable is lower by one means than by another. Even very crude calculation would probably show that this is the case. Under such circumstances a revision of standards could increase the efficiency with which lives are saved or health improved even without specific knowledge of benefits. The entire field of health standards is badly in need of economic research.

Similar calculations of the value foregone are useful in other instances where explicit benefits cannot be estimated: for example, when standards are set to protect the aesthetic value of the environment. Then we are in a position to ask whether the attainment of a certain aesthetic standard is worth at least, say, $50 million. It is a waste of time to debate the adoption of an aesthetic, health, or any other kind of standard without some idea of what must be given up to attain it.

CASE STUDIES OF ENVIRONMENTAL QUALITY SYSTEMS

Once a problem in quality of the environment has been cast into a suitable conceptual framework and empirical measurement of relationships and values has proceeded beyond a certain level, case studies of actual situations can be useful. They may point toward improved resources management procedures and help to develop analytical techniques. Furthermore, they can reveal problems and opportunities not perceived at a more abstract level and provide an improved assessment of the relative significance of various problems.

In the area of water quality, where conceptualization and what we have called supply and demand studies have come some distance, several case studies have been started. The problem they are addressing is to identify the technical alternatives to existing practices and how to utilize them in optimal combinations in view of the social costs and benefits (internal and external, public and private) associated with each. Challenging problems of engineering, economics, and systems analysis are involved. We have already mentioned that where it is not feasible to make explicit measurements of the willingness to pay for particular outcomes, analysis of the measurable costs and benefits associated with achieving alternative levels of control can make explicit the value otherwise implicitly attached to such outcomes. It will frequently take analysis of an extensive geographical area and a complex interrelated system to make such a determination.

INSTITUTIONAL DESIGN

The state of our knowledge concerning appropriate institutions for gauging and managing the external or side effects of resource use is primitive. Problems are emerging and developing so rapidly that gradual institutional adjustment based on a process of unplanned adaption may be very costly, not only in terms of failure to deal with problems but in missed opportunities for using efficient measures to do so.

At numerous points in the preceding chapters the problem of institutional arrangements has been raised in dealing with watersheds, air sheds, urban services and utilities, biological insect controls, systematic production of wildlife, and "internalizing" the results of urban and rural ugliness. We know little about how to design institutions which could systematically search out and implement measures for effective and efficient collective action with respect to these problems. Much less do we know whether institutions should be designed for dealing with them individually or in various combinations, or what the best balance is between authority to directly design and manage facilities on the one hand, and the exercise of control through charges, taxes, standards and the like on the other. In some cases where directly relevant market results are absent and values cannot be imputed from market behavior, we must use political institutions to determine relative preference for various possible outcomes. We need to learn how to design institutions to do this systematically and accurately.

The basic question for institutional studies is *how* to make effective use of whatever understanding is developed of the demand, supply, and systems aspects of environmental quality change. For example, how should we organize to secure the best results? What decisions should be made by legislative bodies? What should be the role of referendum? Should a single agency plan and manage the full range of environmental quality adjustments in a given area or should there be multiple agencies? What is the appropriate regional scope of public co-operative agencies? Do different organizational forms significantly affect the participation of interested parties in the decision process? Should planning be separate from execution? And the possible questions cover a far wider range.

Several general problem areas should be given attention in any study of organization and management techniques—whether of the functioning of current institutions or possible modifications.

1. Institutions must be examined to make sure that significant interrelationships are systematically brought into the decision process.

In all cases there is a question of how thoroughgoing should be our attempt to actually optimize, for it is impossible to take into account *all* the variables involved. While this is widely understood, we do not always act on the basis of an appreciation that adequate study of important variables may be hindered by the attempt to study unimportant variables. On the other hand, it would not be sensible, for example, to take effluents per unit of product of manufacturing firms as given in the design of a water pollution control system, although in the study of some water pollution problems the assumption might be appropriate. Nor would it be wise for the study or the design of transport systems to assume that present locational patterns of housing cannot be changed.

In short, in any particular research study it is necessary to assume many things constant that in fact are variable. But a part of our research and a part of our design efforts must encompass all the important interrelated variables in a problem. At some point the system as a whole must be examined to be sure that important interconnections are not missed.

2. Some of the problems we have discussed involve uncertainty in a major way. Our institutions for decision making should recognize this explicitly. We gain nothing by asking experts to set standards for us when there is no knowledge of the effects associated with different standards—nothing, that is, but an unwarranted sense of security. It is important that the uncertainty aspects of these problems be carried into the public consciousness, for society *may* prefer to insure itself against certain highly undesirable but problematical outcomes.

3. In many problems of the quality of the environment, a spectrum of demands is involved. Some want their neighbors at arm's length, but others like hustle and bustle. Some prefer public transportation, some automobiles. The market system almost automatically insures that every pocket of demand for "private goods" will be served, but when goods are provided by public agencies or when their value and quality is controlled or affected by public actions, special efforts are necessary to insure that organizations are formed and operated in such a way as to take account of minority demands. It is all too easy to neglect them in public decisions.

Similarly, it is better to organize so that a unit producing externalities can make its own decisions on the means used for and the extent of proposed abatement activity. This is feasible where a public agency imposes a charge reflecting the external costs imposed. Systems of charges such as effluent discharge or emission charges and tolls on congested roadways are examples of possible importance. In addition to permitting greater flexibility of individual adjustment than performance standards typically do, these procedures provide funds for the capital facilities to be publicly provided. Research and demonstration projects are greatly needed to develop publicly administered prices as tools for efficient regulation of resource uses which have significant external effects.

4. In view of the great uncertainty attending many decisions on environmental quality, organization arrangements must be flexible enough to adapt to changing conditions. Planning and operation of systems of quality management must be viewed as processes an integral part of which is learning and adaptive behavior.

The institutional aspects of environmental quality have received far less study than have other aspects of the problems we have discussed. This may not be inappropriate since it is our belief that such studies are best grounded upon the knowledge of opportunities available which can result from reasonably thorough study of the natural science, engineering, and economic aspects of the problems. Institutional studies, accordingly, might well be associated with the later stages of case studies. On some problems we are far removed from having the appropriate groundwork for such studies. Nevertheless, the time is ripe for endeavoring to attract the interest of legal, political science, and public administration scholars to issues such as we have raised here.

WHO DOES WHAT?

Government sponsored and conducted research has an indispensable part to play in the total research effort. When a private enterprise imposes cost on others, there is no direct monetary incentive to do research to find a means of reducing the external cost. And even if costs were made internal, say by a system of charges, certain important alternatives would lie outside the capabilities of individuals and private enterprises. Furthermore, some of the more difficult problems are so large or complex that only government can finance and assemble the quantity of specialized equipment and personnel essential to their solution. However, the capabilities of government are limited for several reasons. Among these are the inevitable pressures for quick solutions to immediate problems, the limited objectives of individual agencies, and the necessity for public agencies to avoid involvement in studies which infringe on controversial issues or which may lead to severe criticism of established policies. This means that government programs can perhaps be most effective in (1) determining the physical and biological consequences of side effects and (2) developing technological alternatives to existing resources use practices which have undesirable side effects.

This does mean, however, that fundamental development of organizing concepts, evaluation of the consequences of side effects, research useful for designing systems much different from those in current use, and research on institutional arrangements do not receive the emphasis needed.

The federal government has mounted a massive program in certain areas of environmental quality. A rough estimate of federal expenditures directly related to water quality problems in 1965 yields a sum of well over $20 million. During 1965, over $13 million will be spent on air pollution research and a large new program on pesticides has been started. Each of these programs lays heavy emphasis on scientific and technical aspects.

If our assessment of the limitations of government research is right, we must look to non-governmental research to assume the main burden of developing organizing concepts, of evaluating consequences of side effects, of designing systems much different from those now in use, and of doing research on institutional arrangements.

In some cases, however, the problems are so intractable—measurement is extremely difficult, objectives are not clear—that one cannot see an immediately fruitful mode of analysis. A possible example here is the psychological response to the multitude of stimuli reaching the individual as he moves and works in his particular urban environment.

Here the point becomes to identify those features of housing or transport design that make a difference. Even if the answers to such questions are not very satisfactory at present, it is still possible to proceed by experimentation. It is at this point that demonstration projects may be useful. The critical point is to find a designer, an architect, who is able to conceive a new unity and then to provide the resources for a trial run. For example, an attempt to "unload" certain slum areas prior to redevelopment might be a fruitful experiment. Another example would be to attempt to resurrect deteriorating renewal projects along the lines suggested by Jane Jacobs.

Several arrangements are possible. First, there can be projects of limited scope financed by philanthropic agencies. It might be possible to work out some kind of repayment arrangement, as would almost have to be the case with, say, housing. Second, it might be possible to influence design by contributing the design service to a project in return for the privilege of selecting the designer. There is also a question whether we are learning as much from the results of experiments as we should be. Is there an adequate attempt to assess the results of new design in housing and transport? Do less gifted designers have an opportunity to find out about the best things that are being done? Even more important, do the people who control the purse strings have an opportunity to find out about new design? Are there reliable comparisons of effects available to them?

Because of the number of cities and governmental units in this country, not to mention foreign experience, research into the comparative results of the many attempts to grapple with these problems may be just as rewarding as research directed more closely to analysis of the problems. In these difficult areas, it would be quite an advance to know that certain "treatments" seem to be effective and that others do not, even if we do not understand why.

For Product Safety Concerns and Information please contact our
EU representative GPSR@taylorandfrancis.com Taylor & Francis
Verlag GmbH, Kaufingerstraße 24, 80331 München, Germany